In Spite of Me

In Spite of Me

By
Rene Fuentes

XULON PRESS

Xulon Press
2301 Lucien Way #415
Maitland, FL 32751
407.339.4217
www.xulonpress.com

Unless otherwise indicated, Scripture quotations taken from the New King James Version (NKJV). Copyright © 1982 by Thomas Nelson, Inc. Used by permission. All rights reserved.

Printed in the United States of America.

ISBN-13: 978-1-6628-0050-4
Ebook: 978-1-6628-0051-1

Table of Contents

Introduction

Do I think I'm anyone special? No, in fact, I consider myself to be the lowest of the low. I'm just a regular guy who has made regular mistakes with lots of failures in between.

I always felt like I was a square peg in a round world. I never felt I fit in, even in church or with my own family at times. It blows me away that the Creator of the universe would even think of me, let alone die on the cross for my sins so I can spend eternity with Him.

In Psalm 139: 17-18 David says, "How precious also are your thoughts to me, O God! How great is the sum of them! If I should count them, they would be more in number than the sand; when I awake, I am still with you."

Isn't that amazing? He thinks about me and He thinks about you. Next time you go to the beach, see if you can count how many grains of sand there are? Guess what…you can't!

A massive heart attack followed by a triple bypass caused me to look back at my life and identify times that God in His great mercy and grace came into my life. I've reflected on how He has used all the instances of His involvement in my life to bring me to where I am at today.

I'm reminded of what He told Jeremiah in Jeremiah 31:3, "Yes, I have loved you with an everlasting love; Therefore, with lovingkindness I have drawn you."

The beautiful thing about God's love, is that's it not just for me. Everything I've experienced can be yours as well.

I encourage you to join me throughout this book, and see how in spite of me, in spite of you, He loved me, and He loves you. I encourage you to look back at your own life as you read my story.

I bet you will come to the same conclusion that I have that, in spite of you…He loves you.

It is my hope that in the pages to follow you will see how God was involved in the life of a regular, average and normal sinner who grew up in a one-signal light town in the most southern and forgotten city in the Philippines.

It is my desire that you will see how God showed His love to me as I struggled to find my true identity in this world, and how in spite of me…He was always there and will always be there for you too.

Life presents us with the chance to trust Him more. This means trusting in His abilities, character, power, presence and strength. God does not forsake those who seek Him. I hope that you will seek Him as you learn that my story, can also be your story.

Chapter 1:
The Incident

Surfing has always been my escape and distraction from the pressures of life.

While life, other interests and responsibilities had kept me away from surfing as I got older, I learned to just enjoy the beauty and pleasure of it.

It is not a competitive issue for me anymore. Just being in God's creation is a blessing. In my younger years, it became an obsession and a god. I went through a five-year period where I did not miss more than two days in a row of not being in the ocean.

Even when I would be injured, I would still hurry to get to the beach to watch my friends surf.

Throughout the last 10 plus years I've had the pleasure of sharing the ocean with my son. He was an avid soccer player in his younger years. One summer evening we were alone in the water surfing and watching an incredible sunset.

He turned to me and said, "Surfing is so cool." I knew right then and there that he had surfing fever. At the end of that soccer season, he announced that he was done with soccer after leading his team to victory in the city of Mission Viejo's soccer tournament.

His coach was shocked. I can still remember his reaction when my son said he wanted to quit the team to surf.

Since then, I've enjoyed watching his progress. He used to be the youngest kid in the water at one of the more competitive surfing spots in Southern California.

In the last few years, he has been coaching me, telling me where to position myself and which waves to catch. He has also been telling me that I spend too much time talking to others in the water and sometimes he says I'm like a log, just sitting there.

I just enjoy watching him out on the waves. I often wait for him to catch one before I even catch one for myself. I guess I helped create a monster. I enjoy watching others admire his surfing skills.

I've found myself telling others proudly, "that's my son" after watching him rip up the waves. It was part of my strategy; I was actually hoping others would let me catch a wave due to my son's surfing skills.

I miss surfing with him since he went off to college. However, my eight-year-old grandson is starting to surf. I'm looking forward to spending some time in the water with him as well. Maybe I will even create another monster!

Anyway, as you can clearly tell, surfing has always been a big part of my life. It's always been a lot of fun, but I remember a time when things were not especially easy.

It was an average day. I was walking down the trail to my favorite surfing spot. It was a place very familiar to me for I'd been surfing there regularly since the mid-70s.

It was a nice long walk to the surfing spot. I always preferred walking it rather than riding a bike or skateboard. The walk was a nice warm up and gave me a chance to enjoy the trees and vegetation. I've always enjoyed looking and listening to nature.

One time, I saw a bobcat on the trail. He stopped about ten feet away from me, stared at me and slowly walked away. It was always such a different surfing experience there than at the normal Orange County hangouts.

I felt so thankful for still being able to surf at my age. I was looking forward to easing some of the pressure from the stress I was under. At the time I was dealing with some complications with my family members. My dad had just passed away and I was the trustee of his estate.

It was a nice uncrowded day. There was a nice little north west swell running. Trestles is a famous surf spot made up of a number of surf points in Southern California, Lower Trestles being the most famous. Trestles is known as a surfing destination. You can usually meet surfers from all over the world in the water there. I usually surf between Upper Trestles and Cottons. It was around 1:30 p.m. on December 16th, 2017.

There was a smaller than normal crowd surfing the area that day. I paddled out to surf by myself away from the crowd. The water temperature was 55 degrees, a little chilly for me. I was stoked though to be surfing in my new VISSLA wetsuit which kept me very warm.

After catching a few waves, I started feeling very heavy pressure on my chest. I had never felt that type of pressure before. It felt like a very heavy hand was pushing down on me.

I had no idea what it could be. I had no health issues, or issues with my heart. My mind raced as I worried about what it could possibly be.

First, I thought that it was my weight. I was a few pounds overweight according to my Body Mass Index (BMI). I attributed that to my muscles, since muscle is heavier than fat. At least that's what I told my doctor. However, I always felt those measures to be inaccurate. Then I thought that it could have been heartburn from some fried rice that I ate for lunch.

Regardless, I decided to push the feelings aside for the time being. I caught a few more waves but quickly realized there was something very wrong.

After catching my last wave, I started to paddle out again and found myself really struggling in the white water where the waves were tossing me around. The thing is, the waves were only three to four feet high. I decided to go in, and looking at shore I noticed it was dead low tide. I was going to have to take a long walk on slippery rocks to get in.

I prayed, "Lord, just let me just get to the sand." I started walking in, I thought of just dragging my board in by my leash over the rocks. It would be easier than trying to balance on the slippery rocks holding my board. However, it was a new board and I didn't want to ding it up.

I do not remember how long it took me, but I eventually got to shore. I stared at the deserted beach and then walked ten yards before collapsing on my hands and knees.

I was completely unprepared. I desperately wished for my bike because it was a mile walk back to my car. Unfortunately, I didn't have my phone with me either. I left it in my car since I was always afraid it would get stolen while I would be out on the waves.

I remained on my hands and knees and looked back and noticed a surfer getting out of the water right where I was. He even greeted me and told me that he knew me and always saw me surfing there.

For some reason I asked him his name. He said his name was Yossi, which was the same name as a Rabbi friend I had in Brooklyn. I asked if he was Israeli, and he said yes. Then I asked him to call 911, and he quickly dialed the number.

I turned away from him as the pain on my chest was increasing. I also noticed that my vision was getting smaller. It looked like there was a black frame around my vision and it was getting narrower.

I could hear my new friend giving directions on the phone. "Yeah, you know Trestles by San Onofre?" I laughed to myself thinking they'd never find me.

Suddenly things became strange. He stopped talking, I turned around, and he was nowhere to be seen. Looking back, it was an odd occurrence. He never came over to me to ask how I was. He just remained close to the water while calling 911 and then he just disappeared. He didn't even have a surfboard with him. It was odd to say the least.

I waited a few minutes and thought no one was going to come. I decided that I would need to make the one mile walk uphill to my car. My surgeon told me later that I would have died halfway if I had tried to walk back to my car.

As I got to my towel and started gathering my stuff, three State Lifeguard trucks pulled up, I guess I was the only one in the area!

The lifeguards started talking to me. They asked basic questions. I had a feeling I was in a serious situation because they kept repeating the same questions, meanwhile my field of vision was getting narrower.

They said they would put me in the back of their truck and that they would take me halfway up the hill to the EMTs (Emergency Medical Technicians).

They did not tell me what was wrong. I jokingly asked them if I could take a nap in the back of the truck on the way up the hill, to which they said, "No way!" Obviously, things were more serious than I realized.

As I was laying in the back of the State Lifeguard truck, I noticed several surfers heading down the hill, some I even knew. I wondered what they were thinking seeing a fellow surfer riding in the back of the lifeguard truck. I was worried that they would think I was a kook for not being able to handle the small waves.

As the truck got to the old Pacific Coast Highway bridge, I glimpsed the Camp Pendleton EMT ambulance in the distance. After I got out of the back of lifeguard truck, I had no recollection of what they did to me. However, I can still remember one of them saying "168" but I had no idea what that meant.

They transferred me to the ambulance, and I thanked them (something I still do to this day every time I see them when I go to the beach).

They said they would keep my board and gear at the State Lifeguard HQ and later that day my son picked up my stuff.

Meanwhile my field of vision continued to narrow. As we pulled up to Mission Hospital's Emergency Room in Mission Viejo, I noticed three other emergency vehicles parked in front.

I can still remember commenting to the EMT's "Looks like we are going to have to wait in line?" They said back, "No, you are going right to the front."

After that part, everything was a blur, all I remember is that I was wheeled into a room and as I was wheeled past my EMTs I noticed pretty grim expressions on their faces. I gave them a thumbs up, but I really had no idea what was going on.

When I got in the room there were lots of people waiting for me. I still had my new wetsuit on, and two guys started to cut it. I protested, of course, it was my new winter wetsuit, but then they told me, quite seriously, that this was a life or death matter. They needed to cut it.

I thought about it and noticed my field of vision was getting even narrower. I begrudgingly told them to go ahead.

I still had no idea what they were doing to me. I did wake up twice to throw up though. The first time a nurse said to throw up into what seemed to be a plate, of course it bounced back, and I got it all over my face. It's funny the weird things we remember from traumatic experiences!

The second time I threw up, I heard her mention that I got rice on me. It was the fried rice I had for lunch. I kind of laughed to myself after she said that.

Then I noticed that the surgeon was pushing next to my groin area. At that moment, I passed out.

Chapter 2: The Vision

I woke up surrounded by machines, nurses, and my surgeon. I was in a daze when he started talking to me.

He said, "You just survived the strongest heart attack of any patient I've ever heard of."

He told me I had a 168-troponin level, which signifies the number of enzymes the heart sends out during a heart attack. The level was extremely high. My nurse told me later on that the highest she had ever witnessed was a level of only 72.

That number continues to baffle people to this day. When I shared that number with my heart bypass blog group, they started accusing me of making it up, they said it was impossible to have a 168-troponin level. They said I must have got it mixed up with my heart rate. At any rate, it was an astounding figure.

My surgeon continued to explain that I had a 1 in 500,000 chance of surviving a heart attack that strong. He told me that I was their "Christmas miracle."

He thought that me being in good shape helped me survive the heart attack. Before my heart attack, I was doing 50-yard uphill sprints 2-4 times a week. I also worked out almost daily and had not consumed soda for 20 years. I always remained active.

He said he put two stents in me, and that I had a 100% and 90% blockage and that I needed anywhere from a triple to a quintuple bypass surgery.

This was all foreign to me since I never had any heart issues before. He told my wife, son and son-in-law the same thing while they were in the waiting room. My wife was preparing herself mentally before coming in the room and said she was surprised to see me joking with my nurses when she came in to see me.

My health insurance was with Kaiser Hospital, not Mission Hospital. Kaiser wanted to move me to their heart hospital on Sunset Boulevard in Los Angeles after three days in Mission Hospital's Intensive Care Unit.

My heart attack happened on a Wednesday afternoon so, by early Saturday morning I was in another ambulance on the way to Kaiser Hospital in LA.

As I was laying in the back of the ambulance, I noticed that the EMT was coughing. I thought, "I don't want to catch that cough." So, I turned away and faced the wall of the ambulance all the way to LA until I arrived at 2:00 a.m.

They stripped off all my Mission Hospital gear and replaced it with Kaiser Hospital gear, hospital gown and all. I wasn't quite sure why they did this, but I figured it had to do with the competition between the two hospitals or something.

Someone came into my room from the finance dept at 3:00 a.m. asking for my co-pay. I told them I did not have my wallet, and that I came directly from the beach. She was very insistent, so I told her to call my wife later in the morning.

As if my heart problems were not enough to handle, by Sunday I was coughing and struggling with my breathing.

I had caught that cough I did not want to catch from the EMT in the ambulance. My aunt, a cardiac nurse, her husband, a retired surgeon, my wife, and my youngest daughter were visiting at the time.

We were laughing and having a good time. We listened as my aunt and uncle argued about which treatment would be best for me.

I was laughing and coughing at their argument when suddenly the door opened. A nurse wheeled in a large machine and a doctor entered behind her.

They asked everyone to leave the room immediately because my heart was showing irregularities.

The machine was an Echocardiogram and they wanted to see what my heart was doing. I told them I felt normal outside of the cough; however, I did notice that I was struggling with my breathing every time I coughed.

The next day my cough was worse. I was having a harder time breathing, especially once I started coughing. Despite that, they moved me out of ICU to a recovery room.

It was now Tuesday and at 4:00 a.m. and my nurse told me later that she had heard me coughing. She then came into my room and saw me struggling with my breathing as I coughed.

She said she saw me arch my back, and that she watched my eyes roll back into the back of my head. After that she told me that I closed my eyes and tears came out of them. She said she never saw anyone's eyes roll back like that.

I remember after closing my eyes, I opened them up right away and found myself in a different place. I was no longer in my darkened hospital room.

I was in a bright, golden, incredibly quiet, and peaceful place filled with wispy clouds. It was so bright, but I did not need sunglasses. The peace I felt was over-whelming. It was tangible, I could feel it. I never felt that kind of peace before.

I thought "Man, I was just having a major coughing fit on the outside, in here it is so peaceful." I was descending next to a wall. The wall had on its side golden rounded horizontal bars and there was some type of red inscription on them.

It looked like hieroglyphics. I thought "I think I know where I am, and I never want to leave." I did not even think about life on earth, my wife, kids, or grand-kids. I didn't have any thoughts or regrets.

It seemed like I was there for a while. I remember just looking around and being amazed at the peace sur-rounding me. I kept thinking about how bright, golden, quiet, and peaceful it all was. I was moving but not walking. Instead, it was as if everything was moving to me or around me.

Then, I saw a flowing white robe coming towards me. It billowed up and down in the wind, almost as if someone had a fan on it. I had never seen anything so white. I kept wondering how it could be so white.

Immediately I thought of the transfiguration men-tioned in the Bible. I recalled how the apostles were amazed at the brightness of Jesus' white robes as He was transfigured before them in Matthew 17:2. I also thought of Isaiah 6:1 where Isaiah describes how the Lord's robe fills the temple with glory.

I was focused on looking directly at the flowing white robe as it approached me. I did not even think to look up. Instead, I said to myself, "I know who that is, it's the Lord!"

The next thing I knew, I was sitting on His lap with my back to Him. My legs were hanging off His right leg and He was stroking the back of my head as if I was a small child sitting on the lap of my father.

While I continued to feel a tangible sense of peace, I also felt His incredible love and acceptance in a tangible way. Those feelings were so strong, they practically overwhelmed me. To this day, I really do not know how to explain it.

I felt myself sinking into His chest as He was stroking the back of my head. He did not say anything, and I did not say anything. I was happy to stay there forever.

After a while, I felt Him say without speaking, "It's time for you to go back" to which I simply replied "ok." Looking back, I've always wished I would have said more but it is what it is.

After that I felt myself slide right off His right leg and I started to slowly fall. I felt like I was falling in wide circular turns. I somehow sensed the clouds around me as I was falling.

It was kind of like those dreams we have of falling. Then it seemed like I was accelerating as I got closer to my body. I hit my body on the ground with a hard impact and opened my eyes.

My nurse had both her arms under my back telling me to breath. I told her I was ok, I was not coughing any more, my breathing was back to normal. I told her about the experience I had just had.

I wasn't really sure why, but I asked her if she was a Christian. She told me was, and that she was a travel nurse from Africa.

When I told her what happened, she said she was getting goose bumps. I asked her how long I was out for.

I thought she was going to say one to two hours. She said it was only for sixty seconds or so. I couldn't believe it, it felt far longer to me.

Then I asked her if I died. She said no, and that I was just really struggling with my breathing when I was coughing. She also joked that if I died there would have been a lot more people in the room when I woke up.

So, the Lord gave me that vision of heaven. I saw His long, flowing white robe, I felt His touch, sat on His lap, yet I did not see Him. He spoke to me yet; I didn't hear His voice. But I sure felt His overwhelming love, His peace and His acceptance all in a tangible way.

That day I blacked out another 3 times during a coughing fit while struggling with my breathing. Two of those times I was alone reading in my chair and another time, my nurse started shaking me, and I blacked out while talking with her. Each time I was at peace, and I had no panic because I knew I could go to a better place. At the end of the day, my new nurse said she knew why I was passing out. She spoke with my doctor and gave me Lasix. The next morning, I woke up dehydrated and amazingly, my cough was gone.

I have been telling people about that vision ever since. I must admit that after a while, I started doubting if it really happened or if it was just a dream. People's reactions contributed to this. In fact, most Christians would just roll their eyes when I would tell them the story. On the other hand, I actually received more positive responses from non-Christians.

One day, I ran into a gentleman I knew who lived in my hometown. He was a teacher at a local Christian High School and was also an author who would speak to various Christian groups nationally.

He was very well respected. His father was an accomplished author and still has a thriving worldwide ministry to this day. Anyhow, I told him about the vision I had and asked him for his opinion about it.

As things would have it, the timing could not have been more perfect. He told me was in the process of researching Near Death Experiences (NDEs). He even had three books on the subject in his car.

He told me that my vision was remarkably similar to everyone else's. Mind you, at the time I didn't even know what an NDE was.

However, he explained to me that it had a beginning, middle and an end. Conversely, dreams are never organized like that. Also, feelings in NDE's are strong. The feelings of love, peace and acceptance that I had were so real and overwhelming. They were unlike feelings in any other dream I had.

It was clear, I did not have just a dream, I came close to the brink of death. When I woke back up that in the hospital, little did I know that the vision I had that day would completely change my perspective on life.

Chapter 3:
Under the Knife

During my stay at the hospital I quickly learned that you don't get the chance to get much rest there. Between the hourly blood draws, and nurses waking you up at 5:00 a.m. to start your day I became pretty exhausted from the whole affair. Still, I tried to make the best of it.

I exercised around the corridors of the hospital around 6:00 and 7:00 a.m. each day. I actually looked forward to the walks. All of the folks I raced around the hall with had just completed their bypass surgeries.

Naturally, they were awfully slow, and it wasn't like I was fast either by any means. In fact, they were all using walkers. As for me, since I just had a couple of stents put in, I did not have to use a walker and was very mobile. Being the competitive the guy that I am I tried to burn rubber while pushing my IV in front of me.

One day, my nurse said I was giving everyone a show. I thought she was complimenting me on lapping the field again, but in reality it was her way of discreetly telling me that I forgot to close my hospital gown in the back all the way. No wonder the nurses were laughing at me!

My Kaiser surgeon suggested that we hold off on the bypass for about 3 months. He said my heart attack was so traumatic that clots broke off inside my heart walls.

He suggested I be put on Coumadin which is a blood thinner and that I be monitored for 3 months. The Coumadin would be able to dissolve the clots that developed inside my heart walls after my heart attack. He said that any surgery before then would be too complicated. He did not put me on any dietary restrictions which was nice. He almost gave me the ok to continue surfing those three months then changed his mind, darn it.

So then, a week after my heart attack, on December 23, 2017, I was discharged from the hospital. I asked my wife to bring me some clothes to wear home from the hospital, and she brought over my pajamas.

On the way home, I talked my wife into stopping at my favorite Thai restaurant in Cerritos. It was my parents' favorite restaurant. To this day I always try to stop by when I'm in the area. So, after nearly dying a few days earlier, there I was, fresh out of the hospital, in my pajamas, eating Thai food. In light of everything, I can honestly say that was the best Thai food I had ever had!

As I waited for three months for my triple bypass, life proceeded in a fairly normal fashion. I did zero surfing but was still able to do a lot of walking and I was able to work out at home. However, there were a couple of things that did happen that were important.

First, my general doctor insisted that I get a flu vaccine, which was something I never did. The idea of putting actual germs into my body to fight a disease never made sense to me.

However, she tried to persuade me otherwise. She told me that since I had the heart attack that I needed to protect myself from the flu and from pneumonia. So, like sheep going to the slaughter I dutifully went and got my shots.

In no time I was deathly sick. I think I contracted both the flu and pneumonia at the same time if that is even possible. I could not lay down when I slept, I had to sleep sitting up on the couch for 2 weeks.

Along with my daily Coumadin, I was not feeling too well. One night, I had my normal coughing fit and I stood up too quickly. Next thing I knew I was waking up from the floor with pain in my face and knees. I woke up in a daze, wondering what happened, I did not even know how long I was out for.

My wife came home shortly thereafter, and gave me a weird look, asking what happened. I looked in the mirror, I had a couple of black eyes and bruises on my face.

The next day I met with my Bible Study Group which I had been leading for over 15 years. They all gave me the same look my wife gave me. I just told them

I got in a fight over a parking spot at Costco, and that they should have seen the other person.

I told them that I would have won the fight, but that she got me when she hit me with her walker. It's funny, a couple of the guys actually thought it happened and wanted more details.

I told my doctor about getting sick from the vaccines and fainting, she just nodded and smiled but she did not seem too concerned.

Regardless, my surgeon continued to monitor my tests from the Coumadin treatments. He was happy with my reaction to not only the Coumadin but to the other drugs I was on.

As a result, he decided that March 19, 2018 would be the day for my bypass surgery. Part of my preparation was going to the Kaiser Hospital on Sunset Blvd. and meeting with him before the surgery.

We had a nice talk, he was of Indian decent, he said Indians and Filipinos have the worst hearts in the world. I am Filipino and I think our hearts are worse. For instance, we eat fried pork and rice lathered in the same pork grease from frying the pork. I must admit however that it tastes amazing!

Anyways, most Indians are vegans, and maybe their heart issues stem from all the extra chili they put on their food.

He was very encouraging, and he told me not to worry. He said that his staff do heart surgeries on almost a daily basis. I left the meeting encouraged.

He told me to be at the hospital by 5:00 a.m. and that it would be a 4 to 6-hour procedure. He reiterated that everything would go swimmingly unless there was a complication. I must admit, I was nervous but not worried. For me, the worst thing that could have happened was spending eternity with my Savior.

On the day of my surgery, the drive to the hospital at 4:00 a.m. was surreal. I know both my wife and son were worried and very tired from getting up so early. I told them to just drop me off and go back home.

I knew I was going to be out of it for three to four days and it was such a long drive. Plus, there was traffic and construction on the freeway to contend with.

I was wheeled into the op-prep room. There were four of us going through heart surgery that morning. A nurse had to shave me, then my surgeon and some of his team came by to greet me.

Next thing I knew it was on to the operating room. It was an exceptionally large room and well stocked with stuff on the walls. Before I knew it, the anesthesia had me out like a light. The last thing I remember hearing someone say was "All this is for you."

I woke up in a darkened room. I looked to my left and saw a nurse staring at a machine attached to my body. For some reason I knew it was two or three in the morning.

I started to wonder if the nurse ever fell asleep staring at the screen in such a quiet, darkened room. I know I would. So, I asked her, and she replied with an empathic

"No, you might die if I were to fall asleep!" So, I suggested she drink more coffee and we laughed about it.

The first few days after the bypass surgery were painful. I had Atrial fibrillation (AFIB) which is an irregular heartbeat. It felt like my heart was popping out of my chest. I would not wish AFIB on my worst enemy.

I sensed a lot of activity around me. I was also in a lot of pain. I kept asking for more and stronger pain killers. I had some visitors; I do not even remember what I said to them.

After three days or so in ICU, they moved me to the recovery room. As I got in the recovery room, I think I was still out but conscious. I sensed or saw two very white ghost like creatures swirling around me very quickly.

The best I can explain it is that they were similar to the creatures in the Raiders of the Lost Ark scene when the angels appeared after the Ark of the Covenant was opened. They kept going around me and I sensed joy coming from them.

They would kind of pinch and touch my toes and various parts of my body as they continued to swirl around me. Their touch was cold but not freezing. I had a feeling the worst was behind me. I started wondering how many people died in this room and made a note to ask my nurse in the morning before I fell asleep.

The next morning, I asked my nurse, "So, how many people have died in this room?" She said, "None, by the time the patients get this far, everyone goes home." I thought, "Hmmm, so those were not ghosts that I felt last night." If those were not ghosts, could they have been angels who were sent to comfort me and give me a message that everything will be ok?

My nurse was looking at my report and asked me why I was only taking Tylenol for my pain while in ICU. I told her that I did not know, and that I took it simply because it was what my ICU nurse gave me.

She asked if I wanted stronger pain meds, so I chose Norco which is a mid-strength pain killer, but it works well. I settled into my normal hospital stay routine of getting constantly woken up and waking up at 5:00 a.m. to order breakfast followed by a morning walk routine around the corridors.

This time I was completely humbled as I started my rehab. I went from being the Mario Andretti of the Cardio Recovery Department three months earlier to the cardiac slowpoke.

As I started to walk around the hospital corridor, I had to use a walker. There was this much older and somewhat heavy lady passing me, she was using a walker as well. She deliberately got next to me before turning on her after burners. She turned around, and gave me a little smirk as she left me in her dust.

My nurse this time was a male nurse and when the lady left me in the dust, we looked at each other in shame. He suggested that I pick up the walker rather than pushing it as I moved forward, and his suggestion worked! I was able to go faster but still could not catch my new nemesis as I watched her deftly maneuver around a couple of wheelchairs and gurneys in front of me.

I thought I heard a cackle as she and her nurse disappeared around the corner. I knew I'd have to keep my eye on her. My nurse and I set up a training regimen to make sure she would not do that to us again.

After seven days, I was released from the hospital and no, I never saw my nemesis again. My nurse and I tried to actually avoid her and any further embarrassment to both our manhood's.

I met some great people while in the hospital. I had a nurse who grew up in the church in South Korea who said she had been running away from the Lord for a number of years.

I told her the Lord wanted her back and she raised her arms right there in my room praising God with her eyes closed.

An X-Ray Tech, a Muslim who recently converted to Christianity, said he was retiring and returning to Eritrea to share the gospel with his family back in his country. He said he was not afraid to go back to a Muslim dominated country. We encouraged each other.

Another nurse who worked in the nurse's station volunteered to push my wheelchair after I was discharged. Once we got in the elevator, she asked if she could pray for me, her prayer was so intense and amazing, I did not even know she was a Christian.

The miracle was that our elevator ride was not interrupted all the way down to the first floor from the eight floor. This is amazing considering that Friday afternoons are terribly busy at Kaiser Hospital since they try to release patients before the weekend.

Both my daughter and I could not believe our elevator did not have to stop on the way down. I also had some great fellowship with my male nurse. As it turned out he recently became a Christian and was raising his kids as a single parent.

In spite of me…God was using and blessing me in that hospital.

After my surgery, I had gauze covering my chest and stomach area. On the day of my discharge a doctor came in and removed the gauze revealing wires sticking out of my chest area.

She said they were connected to various parts of my body including my heart. She said they do this in case they have to shock your body. As she pulled out the wires, she pointed to a small fleshy piece stuck at the end of one of them.

She said that it was a small piece of my heart and I asked if I could take it home. She said I was the first patient who asked to take the wires home. I was planning to show the piece of my heart to a friend and to freak him out. To this day, he will not even look at the scar on my chest. It would have been fun to see his reaction.

My surgeon came in to say goodbye and said to me that he would see me in ten years. I found out later, that the mortality rate goes up significantly eight to ten years after open heart surgery.

It sure changes your view of life when you know that you may have a limited time left in this world. However, God is ultimately the one in control.

This is why He says for us "to be still and know that He is God" and that "His thoughts towards us are of peace and not evil, to give us a future and a hope." (Ps. 46:10, Jer. 29:11) He even says to us that "He is able to do exceedingly above all that we ask or think, according to the power that works in us." (Eph. 3:20)

After my heart attack and heart bypass surgery I realized no matter how well I tried to take care of myself that ultimately God is in control. What I just went through showed me I really have no control. I learned, I cannot breathe, take a step, blink my eye or make my heartbeat without the Lord. All I could really control was my attitude in regard to what happened to me.

Chapter 4:
Recovery

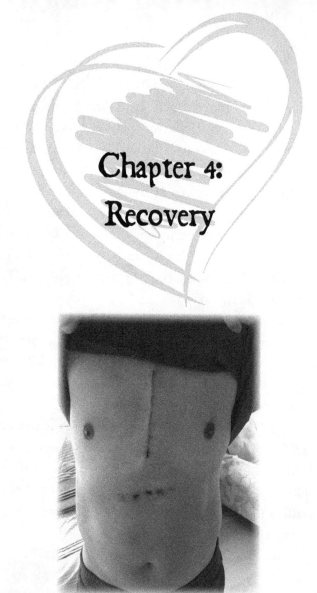

The post-surgery recovery process was quite arduous. I was not allowed to drive. I could only sit in the back seat of a car. I had to consistently take medications, I was not allowed to lift anything over ten pounds and to top it off I had to hug a heart-shaped pillow for the next three months.

In addition, coughing was painful and the routine in general was just very difficult. I was blessed to have my wife stay with me those three months.

She had to drive me everywhere. She helped me take my meds morning and night. I was taking so many different pills, it was confusing. The only pain I experienced and still do today is pain in my left leg. It's the same leg they took veins from to use for the bypass. The pain is still there today, two and a half years later!

I decided to do my rehab at home rather than in physical therapy. I found my regular workout was harder than the hospital therapy, besides by doing my rehab at home, I saved over $200.00 per session. And they wanted me to do over 30 sessions!

My wife and I started walking, which is the best thing for a cardio patient to do. Initially I walked with a walker, but gradually I was able to walk on my own. I could not believe how slow I was and how many breaks I had to take. Just getting from my bedroom to the kitchen felt like a mile.

I should have spent more time understanding the procedure and taking a more active part in the whole process. My surgeon did not go into the details of the surgery so much at our meeting and I did not ask too many questions.

He did not tell me that they were going to cut open my sternum and have it held open for hours, though he did make a faint reference to placing wires to hold my chest together and how my arms would be placed in an unnatural position while they were operating on me.

Today, I still have some shoulder pain. Also, he did not mention anything about the heart and lung machine which was used to keep me alive while they froze my heart so they could work on it.

Later, I found out short term memory loss is a common symptom of using such a machine. In my case, my short-term memory loss is pronounced but it has slowly gotten better. I would forget things that I knew, while at the same time everything seemed to always be on the tip of my tongue.

However, I realized that I might not be able to do the type of work I used to do ever again. I found out more about the procedure and common issues of the surgery and medication after everything took place. I've often blamed myself for not educating myself prior to the surgery.

If you or someone you know has to go through a heart procedure, I suggest you look up inspire.com under bypass surgeries. It's a great site for someone who has questions regarding the procedure. You will get responses from all over the world. I have learned so much post-surgery that I wish I would have known pre-surgery.

As part of my healing, I have forgiven the family members who helped cause my heart attack. After the death of my father on December 2016, my job as the trustee of his trust was to follow his instructions. It was at this point I started hearing comments such as, " You never did anything good for mom and dad," " You don't deserve any money," "You tried to fight dad when you were 12", "You did not even live with us, you lived with grandma" and so on.

I decided to not let it affect me, but it did. I could not believe how much stress those comments and negative attitudes caused me. I decided since to rest on Romans 8:28 where Paul says, "We know that all things work together for good to those who love God, to those who are called according to His purpose."

So, I resigned myself to being a regular heart bypass patient which meant lots of meds, naps, fatigue, daily rehab, weakness, and short-term memory loss. I had to try extra hard to stay positive in that new normal.

However, a year later, I learned I could not even be a regular patient since my reaction to my meds was putting me in a dangerous situation.

Eventually I started getting stronger, though. I set up a goal to go surfing on the one-year anniversary of my heart attack at the same spot where I had my heart attack.

I was diligent with my rehab. The goal of getting back in the water was a good motivator. When the day finally came, I went by myself down to the beach.

It was a nice morning and there were plenty of people in the water. As I got in, I knew I was weaker.

My timing was way off, it did feel good though, to just get wet and paddle out to the line-up.

People asked me where I had been, and I shared my heart attack story. My story hit a nerve with everyone because another surfer recently drowned in the same spot from a heart attack.

He had a heart attack, but rather than getting out of the water, he kept trying to surf. He drowned and was found floating face down later that morning.

It happened on a Saturday morning, there were a lot of people in the water. The guys even said I knew the guy, and that he was another local. They said he was a Filipino surfer, but when they mentioned his name it did not sound familiar.

There are a number of Filipino surfers who frequent the same spot on weekends, they come from all over Southern California. We have spent countless fun times recounting stories in Tagalog (it's the main Filipino dialect). This includes many times where I've tried to fake my Tagalog as best as I can.

That first day back, I ended up mostly telling people about what happened to me. It was like I was telling my story to a revolving door of passersby.

As one guy would paddle away after hearing my story, another guy would paddle up and tell me he overheard the conversation and so I'd start all over again.

A couple of guys even let me have some waves. I think I only ended up catching three waves. Clearly, I had a lot of work to do.

When I got out of the water and walked to my towel, some of the people I spoke with in the water were pointing at me and telling their friends about my experience. I even got some thumbs up.

I told everyone I spoke with to get their hearts checked which I have been doing ever since. Thankfully, I have had three friends that have gotten checked up and that have had stents implanted. I really cannot encourage people enough to get their hearts checked. If you haven't been to a heart doctor ever or in a long time definitely make it a priority.

After that first time, I went surfing another four or five times before the pain around my left knee became so strong that I had to stop. I have been rehabbing that leg ever since. Eventually the pain was so bad that I decided to see a specialist.

I went to an ortho surgeon and he said the pain was due to veins being pulled from my leg during my bypass surgery. I also had nerve damage and iliotibial band (IT band) syndrome on that leg, and I found out I had age-related arthritis starting on my left knee as well.

So, I needed to seriously re-consider the timing of my comeback to the world of surfing. I set a new date for June 1, 2020, and I'm happy to say that since I've been back in the water! I am also pain free after two-and-a-half years of rehab and lots of walking. My rehab consisted of walking 2-3 hours a day and stretching, along with core work for an hour a day 5-6 days a week. And by God's grace, my goal now is to surf three times a week.

During my recovery I had to get off my heart meds due to an inverse reaction to beta blockers that was causing me to have fainting spells. I have hypotension, which means I have low blood pressure. Beta blockers cause your blood pressure to drop, by taking beta blockers, my blood pressure dropped even more. Trying to get up too quickly would thus lead to fainting spells.

The fainting spells caused me to fall on the floor. Fortunately they happened when I was at home. My last fainting spell took place during the end of September 2019 and it was severe. I woke up in a pool of blood and drove myself to the emergency room. I ended up with twenty stitches on my forehead from the fall.

I made an appointment with my general doctor a few days after my fall. She suggested I stop my beta blockers. Today I am on over fourteen different supplements and feel much better. I have also stopped all of my heart medications.

My prior test results were always very good, and I thought the chance of dying from a fainting spell was much higher than the chance of dying from another heart issue. If any future test results would show my heart condition deteriorating, then I would consider getting back on my heart medications. Please don't follow my example in this matter. Please discuss any changes to your medication with your doctor.

Ultimately, the heart attack caused me to reflect back on how God has always been there in my life, even when I was the farthest away from Him.

Chapter 5:
Across the Pacific

God has always worked in my life without me realizing it. As a kid I grew up in a one signal light town in the southern part of the Philippines where most of the transportation consisted of horse drawn carriages, jeeps and tricycles.

Zamboanga City was my hometown. It was known as the City of Flowers and today is home to over one million people.

Traffic congestion, and an influx of Muslim immigrants have made living conditions a challenge for its residents. It is certainly a different city than I remember it to be.

I lived there with my grandma, I was her oldest grandson, and I had lots of cousins. My grandma offered to take me in, and I happily moved in with her. Meanwhile, my parents and three sisters lived in Manila.

I lived in Zamboanga City from second to sixth grade. Sometimes I visited my parents for vacations. In

Zamboanga most of my family lived on the same street. The properties consisted of big lots where there were plenty of fruit trees and even some old US airplane parts from World War Two. It was such a small town that at one time my one uncle was the mayor, a few other of my family members were in the city council and another uncle was the chief of police.

We even had an area in the jungle where we built a club house, individual tree houses, and booby traps. After watching the movie, The Great Escape with Steve McQueen we were inspired to build a tunnel. Our tunnel was 6 feet deep and maybe 10 feet long. My family had a coconut oil business, and we built forts with the coconut husks.

There was no TV which made no difference to me. We could go to the river, rice fields or the beach. We were active in the Catholic Church, and I was a Boy Scout and as such I attended an all-boys Catholic school. We would be out playing all day. We made little toy boats and took them to the river; we made our own bows and arrows using the banana trees for target practice. We made scooters using old rolling skates for our wheels. We made our own slingshots and got so good that we would aim for the stem of a mango high up in the tree. Of course, we did not want to eat a bruised mango.

After watching sword fighting movies, we would make our own swords and shields. We got good at marbles. We created battle scenes on the mud and dirt with our little army men. We played tag for hours. We played basketball on dirt courts. We really did not have a lot of toys, but we made do, and we were never bored. We would even spend hours throwing rocks at targets. We were never hungry, there were so many different fruit trees all over that we did not even bother eating avocadoes, we just let those fall off the trees.

We had chickens, water buffaloes, goats, pigeons and pigs. Once my grandma wanted to go have a party at the beach for some occasion. She had a pig killed and we took the roasted pig to the beach.

There were plenty of snakes. Anytime we saw one, we killed it. Once, I was up on the second story of my grandma's house watching a hen and her chicks below me. All of a sudden, a big snake crawled out of a hole next to our driveway. It reared its head and from above I could see that it was a cobra.

It grabbed one of the chicks and went back into its hole. The hen was fighting it. I told my grandma about it and she had some of the workers kill the snake. A few days later I saw the same hen and thought, "What would happen if I tried to grab one of her chicks?" Soon as I did, she went after me with her claws out aimed for my face. I dropped the chick and ran away.

One day, one of my cousins took everyone for ride in his family Jeep. Being one of the youngest in the group, I remember chasing the Jeep while it was loaded with everyone. As they pulled away from me, they were all laughing and pointing at me.

I remember being bummed as they pulled away, then later that afternoon reports came in that there was a tragic accident.

The Jeep they were in flipped a few times on the road and a friend of ours who was in the front seat died while everyone else ended up in the hospital.

The death of my friend was devastating to me. I was so sad, I remember seeing him in a coffin at his funeral, he was only in the sixth grade.

As I think back, there were a lot of instances growing up when I could have easily gotten seriously hurt or even killed. I could have been swept away by a swift river, I could have fallen off a tree, or been bitten by a snake.

Yet, as it turned out the Lord was watching over me and stopped me from having any serious injuries back then, even though I did not realize it at the time. That was all before I even had a personal relationship with Him.

Being that most of my cousins and uncles I hung out with were older, they liked to teach me their vices. For instance, they introduced me to smoking when I was only in the second grade. I can still remember flushing a pack of cigarettes in the airplane toilet when I came to the US after the sixth grade!

How did we learn how to swim? My older cousins and uncles would threaten me if I did not jump in the water from a high diving board, which was how I learned how to swim. I even saw them throw my other younger cousins into the water if they did not want to jump in. Am I mad at them? No, it was just how things were back then.

They would ask me and another cousin to beat up on people they picked on, if not, we would get beat up ourselves.

When I was around ten, my grandma's driver taught me to drive the family Jeep. One time, I was driving on the main road with my grandma's driver and saw my great uncle on the roadside waiting for a passenger Jeep to pick him up. I thought I was going to be in big trouble.

I asked my grandma's driver, what I should do. He told me to keep driving, and when we passed my great uncle, while he gave me a dirty look, I thought that maybe I'd be spared from him telling anyone about my driving.

However, that night, I found myself in big trouble. What was funny was that it was not for driving at ten years old. Rather, it was for not picking up my great uncle and giving him a ride!

This was all typical boy stuff, I guess. It was a really fun childhood, but I do not think growing up like that could happen in the same way today if I were a kid in today's world.

Things changed dramatically for me when my father decided to move to America. He left us for three years to get established in the United States. He was a civil engineer by trade.

Later, I learned to really appreciate the sacrifices that my parents went through to move to the USA. They didn't have to; they were established in the Philippines, but they made the move to give us kids better opportunities and to allow us to get a good education and ultimately for me to know Jesus as my Lord and Savior.

My mom and sisters moved to Zamboanga with me and my grandma while my dad was in the US. At the end of the sixth grade, it was time for us to pack up and move to America. Back then I didn't want to go; it didn't make sense to me. It seemed so far away, and in reality, it was.

Nevertheless, we made the move in 1969. I can still remember watching the Apollo moon landing at a cousin's house in Manila before we got on the plane.

I was impressed by what the US was doing, and actually, growing up, we all looked up to the US. We admired what it stood for, and we loved its popular culture too. All of us wanted to own a pair of Levi's and drink Coke.

Plus, we loved American movies. Since I had no TV growing up, we would often visit one of the seven different movie theaters in town. As a matter of fact, going to the movies was a pastime for the entire city.

Once we arrived in America we settled down in La Mirada, California. Our house was just five or six houses down from McNally Junior High, which would be my new school.

So, there I was, "Fresh of the Boat" or FOB for short. Everything was so different; it truly was a culture shock. I remember going to see a counselor and going over what classes I wanted to take for my 7th grade year.

I picked choir first since everyone sang in my all boys Catholic school back in Zamboanga, you did not have a choice. The counselor said, you don't want to do that here. He said it was not cool to be in the choir.

When school started, I quickly realized that I was the only Filipino kid in the whole school. Everyone looked so different from what I was used to in my previous life, which only consisted of brown kids with black hair.

I was particularly blown away by a kid with red hair and red eyebrows, and I just had to write a letter back to my family in Zamboanga telling them about this red-haired kid.

The most amazing thing, however, was that there were girls at my school. I never saw girls in school before. I was slowly trying to figure things out when one day a big eight grader walked up to me and asked a question that caused my life to flash before my eyes.

He wanted to know if I was a lowrider or a surfer. As I studied him, his fists clenched, I knew the wrong answer would result in my first beat down in the US.

I believe the Lord showed great mercy and grace upon me that day by having me ask the kid the same question in response. He proudly said he was a lowrider and I said, "So am I" just as proudly as he did.

Despite a narrow escape from a beating, as I walked away from him, I knew I had to figure out what in the world he was talking about.

I found out that lowriders were typically Mexican kids. This kid was a white kid; he did have his hair combed back. I noticed all the lowrider kids had their hair combed back. I knew I didn't want to be a lowrider since I had a big forehead. I never wanted to comb my hair back and expose my big skull!

While it's a funny example of me trying to understand a new language and culture, there were a lot of other challenges too. For example, simply learning what to call things was a challenge, along with learning how to play football and how to talk to girls.

At the time, I did not consider being required to speak English in my Catholic school in Zamboanga would benefit me so much in the US. If we got caught not speaking English on school grounds, we had to pay a .25 cent fine which we used for a party at the end of the school year. Looking back, being required to speak English in school was very helpful for me in my first few years in the US.

No matter the challenges though, I was so happy to be in America, and looking back God was truly on my side through it all and in spite of me.

Chapter 6:
Antics

By the eighth grade I was figuring things out. I made second string on the junior high school basketball team too. One of my good friends was the star of the team. He thought he was Pistol Pete Maravich.

I tried to go out for the other teams too, but I was too small for football, too slow for track and as for baseball well, forget about it. So, I signed up to be the manager of those teams, which allowed me to leave my classes for all the school events.

One of the other things I remember from those days in La Mirada happened in the ninth grade. A good friend of mine who was also my next-door neighbor came by on a Sunday morning after church wearing a suit and carrying a Bible.

I do not know why, but I made fun of him for carrying the Bible. I still remember the hurt look on his face. Sadly, I never saw him carrying a Bible again.

We lost track of each other for 40 years, in that time, he became addicted to meth. He lost everything and his wife asked him to leave their home and he moved back in with his parents. It's crazy because today I've found myself trying to convince him to read his Bible again.

While in ninth grade we decided to have a sleep over at my house with no more than five friends. We were going to experiment with drinking for the first time. We did not know it at the time, but it was going to be sort of a coming of age party.

One of the guys spent two weeks stealing a little bit of liquor daily from his parent's liquor bottles. The rest of us spent two weeks standing in front of the liquor store asking for people to buy us beer and Strawberry Hill (not a good combination).

Well, the big night finally arrived. As you might expect we acted just like immature ninth graders running around the neighborhood smoking, making prank calls, and throwing up. We were out of control but of course we sure thought we were cool.

I discovered that I turned bright red and broke out in hives and was a total light weight when it came to drinking. I found out later that I'm actually allergic to alcohol, but of course I didn't let that stop me for many years.

The funny thing about the party was that, even years later, all these other guys from school claim they were at the party. I think the number is now up to twelve people!

I planned on playing football my freshman year, but I missed "hell week." When school started, I saw my football coach and said I was ready to play football. My coach said I since I missed "hell week" I would not be able to play. He cited some league rules that said a player who missed "hell week" had to miss so many games in a season.

"Hell week" was a one-week period when you had 2 practices a day. The coaches worked their players very hard usually in the hottest days of the summer. Why did I miss hell week? I started to go to the beach.

He suggested I go out for cross-country, but I didn't know what cross-country even was. However, he said it would help me in basketball, so I went out for cross-country.

So, the day came for my first cross country meet. I do not even remember going to practices prior to my first meet. I threw up during my first meet (I learned it's not a good idea to eat chili cheese dogs for lunch the day of a meet) and passed out on my second.

Nevertheless, I got back up and finished. At the time I was the worst runner on the team. I'm sure my football coach was happy with his suggestion, but as it turned out he would be my basketball coach too!

For practice sometimes a fellow runner and I would hitch hike since we spent much of our time training by running on the streets. One time the school cheerleaders picked us up.

There we were two little freshmen in a varsity cheerleader's car. We suggested they drop us off before we would reach the school. We didn't want to come ahead of the rest of the team since some of them were league champions.

Despite the initial challenges, by the end of the season I was the fifth runner for the team and was lettered. That was my first and last year in cross country though.

After the ninth grade, my parents bought a house in Cerritos and it was time to move away from my buddies in La Mirada as new adventures awaited me.

I made some good friends in La Mirada. In fact, many of us still keep in touch. They were helpful in showing me how to survive junior high and the ninth grade. They really helped me learn how being a kid in America worked along with some adopted cousins who arrived in the US a few years before me. I'm forever grateful to them for that.

That summer when we moved into a new tract of homes, I got to meet and play football with my new neighbors. We played a lot of football. I got used to yelling at them and became comfortable hanging out with them even though they were much bigger than me.

When school started, we all had to take a bus and we shared a campus with another high school until our school, Cerritos High was completed the next year.

My neighborhood buddies turned out to be the tough guys of the school. They would beat up kids on the bus. I'd watch them daily chase this one kid in particular away from the bus. I felt so bad for him.

The leader of the tough guys was so bad that once he asked me and another friend to follow him outside during a basketball game. Fortunately for me, our friend was walking right behind him when the tough guy turned around and hit our friend in the mouth.

We both asked the tough guy why he did what he did. He told us that he just had to hit somebody, and we all walked back to the game as if nothing happened.

There was a lot of tension that year because of just two guys. Namely from my neighbor tough guy and another guy who led the local lowrider gang.

To the school's credit, the school got rid of them both and just like that, the tension was gone. It was like a black cloud was lifted from the whole school; it was amazing.

Eventually I played guard and started for our sophomore basketball team. We played really well as a team. Of course, the more we won, the cooler we thought we were.

This caused us to get way too self-confident in ourselves. As a result, during one tournament, which we were supposed to win, we played so bad because we did not take the other team seriously or respect them.

At halftime our coach was understandably mad. He did not talk to us and made us run lines. Running lines was typically done in practice when the coach wanted to wear us out.

We would run from the baseline and then touch a line further out on the court and then run back to the baseline. This would go on and on until we eventually sprinted from baseline to baseline.

The whole gym quietly watched us run back and forth the whole halftime. It was embarrassing, but we beat the other team the second half. Sometimes there's nothing like a little negative motivation.

After that year, our team stuck together, and we played at the local park that entire summer. Then one day, this big kid came by and introduced himself. He said he wanted to meet us and that he was transferring to our school.

He was at least 6'4" and he said he played point guard. I was amazed because I was only 5'9" and played point guard. This kid became all league, got a college scholarship and became the head coach at UCLA. While he was a nice guy, my basketball dreams got shattered that day.

In fact, towards the end of that summer, we all decided to not go out for the basketball team. Why? We wanted to grow our hair long, start surfing regularly and experiment with drugs.

The guys told me it was my job to tell the varsity coach. When the first day of practice for the basketball team arrived, four of us, all starters from the prior year along with our second-string center, decided we were not going to play.

I spent my time avoiding the coaches at school until one day I heard my name on the school intercom telling me to report to the office. When I got there, I was told that our varsity coach wanted to talk to me.

So, we talked, and I told him we wanted to be hoodlums and do drugs…not really. I just told him we didn't like his haircut rule, and that we had to wear gold game day coats and ties and he said ok. We shook hands and that was that. I guess he knew that he had much better players than us coming on board.

I had him as a teacher for a couple of classes after that and he always picked on me. It was always, "We will be doing speeches, any volunteers, Fuentes?" and "I need a carwash and a car wax, any volunteers, Fuentes?" and so on!

After I while, I did not mind being picked on. In fact, I enjoyed watching the rest of the class suffer after doing my speech. I liked it; I didn't have high expectations to compete with. Kids in high school sure freak out when it's time to give a speech.

After that, I always volunteered to be first in almost everything, even today I do the same thing. In the long run he actually became my favorite teacher.

I did play for a church team that season. I did not have to get a haircut. We lost in the state championship game in Oakland. And I made the all-tournament team. That was fun.

I took to my newfound role as a long-haired surfer druggie partier with great enthusiasm. We surfed, partied and experimented every chance as if making up for lost time.

One day, I met with one of my old basketball coaches who was also my counselor and asked him if I could start school later in the day. He asked me why, I told him I wanted to go surfing in the morning.

He stared at me, signed my new schedule and told me not to tell anyone. I walked out of his office on cloud nine and told everyone I knew. My new school schedule became, wake up at 4:00 AM, drive to the beach, be home by 9:30 AM and start school at 10:00 AM. Go back to my house for lunch with friends, party, back to school by 1:00 PM high as a kite.

After school I would go to work at a car wash, most of the guys there were surfers with long hair from different schools in the area. We would get together and party again that night and start all over again the next day. I had to take stimulants to keep up with such a demanding schedule.

I remember finding a Bible at of one of the parties I attended. It was the first time I ever picked up and opened a Bible, I tried to read it while drunk and I thought it made sense to me.

We tried everything available. Once after taking some pills my friend gave me, we both had to go to the bathroom, and we started screaming when we noticed our pee was bright red. We took some pills that had red food coloring in them.

I actually thought that we were being really dumb by taking stuff that we didn't know anything about.

By the middle of my senior year, I was getting tired of partying at my house for lunch. Things were getting bad. Guys were beginning to steal alcohol at the store, and they would come over wanting to stay all day at my house.

As a result, I started to stay at the beach instead of going to school. I wrote my own notes, but I quickly ran out of excuses. Once I wrote down that I was absent due to extreme fatigue.

There were a lot of other things we did that easily would have gotten me in big trouble. Looking back, it was God's mercy and grace that saved me from all of my dumb choices.

Today, a majority of my high school party buddies have come to a saving knowledge of Jesus Christ as their Lord and Savior. However, others are also dead.

When my kids were still little and we were watching TV, alcohol commercials would come on and show these perfect people in cool settings drinking spirits. I always made the comment that they should show another commercial showing those people's lives 10-20 years later when their perfect bodies become bloated and diseased and when their lives are a mess.

If you are considering or experimenting with drugs or alcohol, please don't do it or get help to stop.

In 2008, I started a business that provided qualified leads to the rehab industry. It was the first of its kind.

We created a commercial which showed this young housewife talking about how her partying lifestyle led to addiction and her family being torn apart.

We bought empty cable slots across the country and showed the commercial after 12 AM. Every time we showed the commercial our call center was overwhelmed by calls of desperation from people from every market demographic.

We recorded all of the calls, and I would listen to people crying for help, seniors becoming addicted to pain medication, adults with ruined families and lives and even 16-year-old kids wanting to stop smoking.

The business had to shut down, it was difficult raising capital in 2008 since it was the beginning of our last recession. But it did show me the effects of drug and alcohol addiction. Like those alcohol commercials, it looks cool at the beginning but if you keep it up, before you know it, you are addicted.

Drugs are much more powerful and addictive today even than when I was experimenting with them in the 1970s. I believe they are one of the most powerful tools the devil has in his arsenal.

In the John 10:10 it says, "the thief does not come except to steal, kill and to destroy. I (Jesus) have come that they may have life, and that they may have it more abundantly."

The devil is that thief and he uses drug and alcohol addictions to steal, kill and destroy lives.

Chapter 7:
Days of Surf and Snow

After graduating from high school, I had no real plans or goals. I remember a girlfriend's father asking me what my future plans were. I told him that I wanted to find an island in the Philippines and surf and live there the rest of my life. Obviously, he did not want his daughter to go out with me and in retrospect I don't blame him.

Unlike surfers today like my son who has been to Indonesia and Nicaragua to surf, my friends and I mainly surfed in Baja, California. A friend of mine spoke Spanish like me and together we would often go surf our favorite spot in Mexico called K55.

It was called that because it was 55 kilometers from the US/Mexico border. Today K55 is being developed and is closed for public use. Sometimes we would venture another 150 miles south of the California and Mexico border.

We knew the family who kept guard over the place, they had a little place at the spot. We would always bring clothes and canned goods for them when we stayed there. Since my friend and I worked together and had the same days off, one summer we went there every week.

There were no facilities, no showers, water or bathrooms. It was just a barren dirt hill with no grass or trees overlooking a pretty fun surf spot.

I don't know why we never brought sleeping bags, tents, water or other necessities. It was not just us, back then if you went down to Mexico you usually wanted to bring someone who spoke the language.

I was usually asked to go on lots of trips, and no one brought tents, sleeping bags, or water on them either. Even when running into other guys we knew; it was the same thing. You were lucky if someone even remembered to bring their towel.

After surfing all day, we would bake in the hot sun with no shade while being attacked by sand flies. We did not even bring hats or sunglasses. Warm beer was the solution to our thirst and to overcoming the heat.

I remember brushing my teeth with beer. Remember, I'm allergic to alcohol! In the evening it was the same thing, we would sit around the campfire, and we would just end up sleeping wherever we landed.

One trip a friend woke up next to the campfire with ashes all over his face and tongue. One morning I woke up with a mangy, hairless, flea bitten dog licking my ear. As you can clearly tell, it was high living!

On another trip, we got to a nice surf spot in the dark after getting stuck in some mud all afternoon. Of course, we didn't bring any wood to start a fire. So, everyone started searching for firewood.

A little local kid showed up and said that some of the guys were taking wood off of his parents' house. They were removing wood that was part of the wall in their house.

It was amazing that none of us ever fell off the cliffs. Nor did we ever get arrested or hurt in the water. We also somehow avoided getting in car accidents or hurt in the canyons when we would look for a bathroom. God had to be protecting me through all those times.

Eventually, I decided to go to junior college, but I thought the girls at another junior college were cuter, so I transferred to that junior college instead of my first pick. Clearly, my priorities concerning education were not important to me back then.

Anyway, I was able to squeeze a four-year college degree out to seven years. During college I continued to surf, but I did not party as much.

I also took up skiing and tennis. When I transferred to a university in 1980, the tennis coach actually asked me to try out for the tennis team. I thought about it, but it was going to be my junior year and I did not have any previous coaching from a tennis instructor. Plus, I was developing tennis elbow, so I declined.

Skiing was a sport I really enjoyed though. The scenery was so beautiful. It caused me to really think about how the beauty of nature could not happen by chance.

The snow, trees, rocks and mountains fit so perfectly together that even the best landscaper could not have put it together so perfectly. There had to be a Creator who created it in all of its beauty and splendor.

I struck a friendship with my economics professor in junior college. One day he asked one of my female friends to go sailing with him and she asked me if I could go with her, but I declined.

This professor used to play with his Mercedes key chain in class. I am sure he dated a number of his students. We ended becoming good friends.

Once, he asked if I wanted to go skiing in Lake Tahoe. I told him I had an accounting final, so he asked who my professor was, and he worked it out for me to go skiing with him. I didn't have to take my final until after the semester.

I enjoyed skiing with him. In the summer he skied on one of the glaciers in South America, same place the US Ski Team practiced. I learned a lot about skiing from him.

I went skiing every chance I got. Once my cousin and I went skiing. We were in his car and our other friends were in another car following us.

We were on the freeway and it started snowing. We got so excited, but I noticed that all the other cars around us slowed down while we started going faster.

Next thing I knew, we started sliding and the car was headed for a cliff! I looked at my cousin and he was frozen in fear. His hands were completely off the steering wheel, so I grabbed it and turned us away from the cliff.

The car started doing a few 360 degree turns, and we ended up in the far-right lane facing traffic. We easily could have done some flips.

Thankfully, everyone just drove by very slowly and looked at us. Once we got to the ski resort, I asked our friends if they saw what happened. They said we were just showing off. I remember rolling my eyes and just being grateful for being alive.

Another time some friends and I decided to go skiing in Crested Butte, Colorado. I was driving a Volkswagen van through Utah early in the morning and snow was on the ground.

Everyone was asleep in the van. I was headed downhill and must have hit some ice. The van started careening from one end of the road to the other. Being in a Volkswagen van without a nose, the side of the mountain on either side seemed to come up very close.

I kept yelling "Whoa!" every time I had to turn the wheel away from the sides of the hillside. This continued during my entire crazy trek all the way down the slope.

The van ended up stalled across the road at the bottom of the hill. By then everyone was awake, and our skis and other belongings were scattered all throughout the van.

The person in the front seat and I looked at each other and grinned a nervous smile to each other, but we made it. Then we looked up and there was a semi barreling down the hill. I knew he was not going to stop, and that he would end up doing what we did.

He laid on his horn, but our van was stalled and was sticking out into his lane. All we could do was watch. The driver and I had eye contact with each other as his truck flew by missing us by inches. After that, my friends did not let me drive the rest of the trip and I didn't blame them!

I had no direction in college. I was always changing majors until I finally settled on marketing. I had an uncle in banking who always told me that marketing people always seemed happier than the other people in the office. So, I thought why not go for it.

I was still going to mass by myself, I usually just sat outside after the doors were closed and would spend my time talking and hanging out.

After a while, I had a desire to get more from church. I decided to actually stay inside the church foyer when mass started, but I still felt that something was missing.

I started sitting in the pews, and over time I even moved up towards the front of the church until finally,

I found myself in "grandma territory" a couple of pews from the altar.

Yet, I still was not getting whatever it was I searching for. I learned later that holiness is not the way to Jesus Christ, rather Jesus Christ is the way to holiness.

Still, I did not know that then. All I knew was that I wanted more out of my life and I felt there had to be more. I just didn't quite know where to look or what it was exactly that I needed.

However, something soon happened that changed my entire perspective and that solved the longings I so badly wanted answers to.

Again, in spite of me God was orchestrating details in my life to draw me closer to Him. I'm sure just as He has with your life. In James 4:8 it says, "draw near to God and He will draw near to you." It's a verse that has resonated with me over and over throughout my life.

Chapter 8:
Success without Fulfillment

One night a girlfriend of mine broke up with me. I told my friends that she took me to watch the old German submarine movie, Das Boot, and they knew that meant she gave me das boot!

Anyway, an old girlfriend felt bad for me and took me to Calvary Chapel Costa Mesa. I was blown away by the message, even more I was blown away by the number of pretty girls there.

As I was standing there, another girl I did not recognize came up and said she knew me from high school. She said she used to pray for me, and my friends and that she was so happy to see me at church.

Rather than thanking her, I thought "I wasn't that bad back then…?" That way of thinking throughout my life kept me away from accepting Jesus Christ as my Lord and Savior much sooner than when I actually did.

As such, thinking that I didn't need a Savior because I was "not that bad" held me back from experiencing many of the blessings of Christ earlier in life.

Compared to others, I thought that I wasn't that bad. However, compared to Jesus Christ, who is our Standard, I was the worst of sinners. The Apostle Paul said he was the "chief of sinners" in 1 Timothy 1:15 and if the Apostle Paul thought that of himself, what was I?

I kept going to Calvary, and I even actually said the sinner's prayer. I also read the Bible and put a Christian sticker on my car, but I did not change anything else.

It's hard to talk about Jesus to your friends while you're drinking at the bar and scamming women. There were plenty of times when I walked up to my car drunk after a wild night at the bar, and I'd notice my fish sticker on my car. I never even thought about what a terrible witness I was to others.

I should have taken the sticker off. I sure acted holy in church though. Once I was driving on the freeway, and another car pulled up next to me. The people were holding up the one-way finger and smiling, I thought they were flipping me off so, I flipped them off. They just gave me this sad look. I guess they noticed my Christian sticker.

In the end I was not saved. Even though I thought I was I was merely a "CINO" which is short for Christian in Name Only. (I just made that up)

At last, after 5 years in junior college, I transferred to a university as a marketing major and of course I spent my junior and the first half of my senior year as a goofball. I thought I did not need to join a fraternity and that I could be my own fraternity.

Again, I wasn't taking anything seriously. Surfing, skiing, girls, bars and tennis were always more important than what really mattered. The worst thing was that in spite of all of this I thought I was a Christian.

That attitude got me in so much trouble. I failed a computer programming class and received a note which said I was kicked out of school. I was to meet with my school counselor and discuss options.

The night before my meeting, I actually prayed to God. I did not want to quit school even though I did not deserve to be there. The next day, I sat with my counselor and he looked me up on his computer and said that there was no record of me taking the class in question.

He suggested that if I was worried about that class, to take it at the local junior college. I walked out of there thanking God for about five minutes but after that I was back to my old self in no time.

That summer I went to a junior college to take the computer class I failed. One of the girls in the class became a friend and said she had a friend that she wanted to introduce me to. Well, her friend became my wife a few years later! It's funny how God works things out.

I was working as a waiter at this time and met a rather interesting person. He was a height challenged person who was an actor, I remember seeing him in some TV shows. He introduced me to two young guys who had their own business training people on unleashing their potential.

I met them, and they were an impressive group of guys. They suggested I read a book called *Think and Grow Rich*.

I was totally impressed. Finally, there was some direction for my life. They told me things like "What you can conceive, you can achieve!"

I thought that the world was my oyster. Of course, I just had to learn how, so I signed up for the course they were teaching. I was such a good student, they asked if I wanted to join the business, which I happily did.

Meanwhile back in college, I was in the middle of my senior year and thought about what would happen if I really applied myself, instead of trying to cheat or charm my way through school.

To my surprise, I got A's my last semester. Now, there were some electives, like, Comic Spirit. But hey, some of those electives were harder than my core classes!

I graduated in 1982 and with my degree in hand and my new way of thinking, I was ready to conquer the world. I thought I could do anything that I set my mind on.

Of course, I could not find a business job after graduating, but I didn't mind. I was busy feeding my mind with tons of self-improvement ideas. I learned how to dress, act, eat, speak, and use my mind all to get what I wanted

I was visualizing, self-affirming and meditating my way to success. I was even developing a self-improvement library and was working with my friends teaching classes on self-improvement which included visualization and positive affirmations.

I also joined Toastmasters to become a better speaker, and I took up speed reading and anything else that would help me be the best I could be.

At one point I would track and review my day in fifteen-minute increments. I had daily, weekly, yearly, and ten-year goals complete with pictures.

I even started going to a fortune teller at her home. She actually had a Bible on her coffee table which looking back was kind of odd, but I digress.

She was not weird; she was just an average suburban housewife. She even wanted to train me, she said I had a "gift." That comment kind of scared me. Going to a fortune teller was highly recommended by a mentor of mine at the time who said that the DuPonts all had their own fortune tellers.

My mentor was a highly successful Wall Street trader who decided one day to chuck it all. He had plenty of money, so he moved to India and studied under a guru.

He came back to teach at college and was impressed by my desire for self-improvement and success. I told him I wanted to go to New York City and be a stockbroker.

After all, I thought that if you could make it there, then you could make it anywhere.

He said he knew all the spots and the people and that he would introduce me to everybody. I felt I was on my way to no longer being average and ordinary. I was the captain of my ship and the ship was leaving the dock.

A strange thing started happening during this time. A small, dark, furry, and very evil being started visiting me at night while I was in bed. I could sense his presence coming from down the street and before I knew it, he would be on top of me with an evil grin trying to choke me.

I remember a dark and sinister presence with small hooves. We would spend what seemed like all night fighting. I'd wake up sweating and tired. I was determined that whatever he was, he was not going to kill me.

I did not realize that all my efforts of self-improvement opened the door to the occult. I was into new age philosophy, yet I still thought I was a "good" Christian.

All of this focus on self was making me very prideful, selfish, greedy, and entitled. All I thought about was me and accomplishing *my* goals. If you stood in the way, I did not need or want you. I learned to act on instinct, and on whatever my heart told me.

The Bible says that the heart is desperately wicked, and it was no wonder that those quick self-centered decisions I was making were pushing me away from the Lord.

Around 1984, I started a new business in the financial services space. It was a lot of hard work but I didn't mind it.

I wanted to start a one-stop financial center. I felt it was me against the world and I used that to motivate me. I worked six days a week, leaving early and staying late. Come Sunday I was a vegetable spacing out in front of my TV.

I experienced some success. There were trips to Europe, a Mercedes and a house close to the beach. My soon to be wife was going to school for nursing and I told her to stop her education. I thought that my business was going to take off, and that she would not need to work.

With my new age thinking, I was also very arrogant and prideful. I viewed people as steppingstones to my goals.

I got married in 1987. After getting my first Mercedes, I told my wife, "From now on, we're only going to drive Mercedes'." I'm surprised a lightning bolt did not hit me right after that comment.

1 Timothy 6:10 states "for the love of money is a root of all evil, for which some have strayed from the faith in their greediness and pierced themselves through with many sorrows."

In 1989, my first of four beautiful children were born. Yet, despite everything, I was never happy. I was never satisfied or thankful. I thought there was an advantage to never being satisfied. I never enjoyed my successes, there were always more dragons to slay. I remember wondering when it would ever end. I knew that the Bible talked a lot about joy, but it never tied joy into circumstances.

Around 1989, while doing one of my positive affirmation sessions, I started thinking about where my way of thinking and believing would lead me. I wanted to know what the end game would be.

I was proclaiming to myself that I was in control, yet having my own business made me realize that there were so many things out of my control. In addition, things happened regardless if I tried to meditate them away or not.

I started to realize that my way of thinking would lead me into believing that I was my own god. There was a lot of pressure in trying to fake it until I made it. New age beliefs involved a lot of "I" and "Me" decisions, and they were always based solely on my wicked heart.

What is more they were bearing bad fruit. After paying everyone I had no money left, and it seemed like I had a hole in my pocket. I was making money, but it went right though my hands.

I was getting accolades, I was paying for nice prizes for sales contests, yet the harsh reality was that I was barely making it. I needed something more than what the life I was living was giving me.

Chapter 9:
Closer to the Truth

One day after going in the office early and doing some paperwork, I left and on my drive home I found a Christian station on the radio. I became hooked on the station and listened to it for the rest of the day.

I continued to listen to it day after day for a year. I also started reading the Bible. As time went by, I felt that the Lord wanted me to get out of the business I was in.

I stopped doing my positive affirmations and laid off the new age stuff. I was looking at my business and thought I would have to continue at my current pace for at least another five years before I could take my foot off the gas.

I did not think I would survive for another five years, plus I did not like the person that I was becoming. My health was also suffering.

One day my mom saw me and asked if I was ok. She said I didn't look well and told me another thing that disturbed me. She said she used to take me to the local witch doctor when I was a baby because I cried too much.

My mom is known as a saint around her friends and here she was telling me that she used to take me to a witch doctor. No wonder my fortune teller thought I had a gift!

I decided I was willing to lose the business, the house, my car and everything in order to get things right with God. After seven to eight years I thought it would be nice to be a regular nine to five person.

I didn't want to be in the front anymore. I wanted to come home, play with my family, go on regular vacations and have regular weekends.

I thought that maybe being average and ordinary would not be so bad. While I was yearning to be in the "back row" in the back of my mind I thought God would put me in another situation where I would be a success and where I would be prosperous. Little did I know what God had planned for my family and me.

I was afraid what my wife would say, so I prayed for guidance. After a year of driving around listening to Christian radio and reading the Bible, I told my wife that I was getting out of the business scene I had become so entangled in.

She was actually happy, and she told me that she never even liked the line of work I was in anyway. My jaw dropped to the ground. She liked the goodies that came with it but not the business itself.

Another thing happened to me after this. I finally realized I was a sinner. I was not a good guy, nor was I a guy who was "not that bad." I was a sinner and I desperately needed a Savior!

I told the Lord I was a sinner and that I needed Him to save me. But deep down, there was something that still said that I was not that bad, that I deserved success and that God would give me all of my wants if I worked hard enough.

I still had not come to terms with myself, even after reading the Bible and learning that my best was nothing more than filthy rags. Even after learning that there was no good thing in me, and that my heart was desperately wicked.

I still lived to please myself which was and is the ultimate form of disobedience to God. We must live for His approval and not for our own approval or the approval of others.

"For you were once darkness, but now you are light in the Lord. Walk as children of light. For the fruit of the Spirit is in all goodness, righteousness, and truth, finding out what is acceptable to the Lord." (Eph. 5:8-10)

Pleasing God by doing His will is an internal matter of the heart but I had to figure out if I was really interested in doing His will in my life.

I started to think of all these great things that I could do for God, but the truth was they were all things I wanted to do for my own glory and not God's.

God's plan for us is about building eternal treasures in heaven. It's not about building our own kingdoms here on earth. I had to also ask myself if I wanted to be a blessing, or just be blessed.

Here we were with a big mortgage and various expenses, and I had no job. I thought I didn't have to worry about anything because God was going to help me.

We started going to church and this time I actually listened to the messages. However, I could not find a job, and after one year we had to move out, and turn my Mercedes in. What is more, I was about to make one of the biggest mistakes of my life.

There were a few verses that stuck with me through this time. If you draw near to Me, I will draw near to you (James 4:8). What good is it to gain the whole world if you lose your soul (Matthew 16:26). What is highly esteemed by man is an abomination to the Lord (Luke 16:15).

Just what was that big mistake? Well we moved into my parents' house and I told my wife we should just move into an apartment, but she was panicking. I thought we should trust God.

So, we agreed this would be a very temporary move. I believed God wanted us to trust Him however we were showing Him that we did not trust Him. By not trusting in the Lord in this situation, I thought we were terrible witnesses to our family and friends. Even though we helped my parents by paying rent and expenses, I still thought it was the wrong move.

God's work in our lives depends upon His promises to us, not our promises to Him. God does His most beautiful works in our valleys.

There we were, my wife, daughter and I sleeping in my old room at my parent's house. I wanted to walk with the Lord, I knew He had forgiven me, but I was struggling with His forgiveness.

I just could not believe that He would accept my past. I struggled with this for months until one night I had a dream.

I was watching someone digging a hole for a while and for some reason I knew it was the Lord. I asked Him, "Lord, what are you doing?". He stopped digging, turned to me, and said, "I'm digging a hole and then I'm going to put all your sins in it and cover them up." As soon as He said this, I started crying in my dream, and I woke up and had tears in my eyes.

I finally got a job working as an investment counselor for a bank. My wife went to work cleaning houses for the same person who used to clean our house. One day at the bank a business acquaintance from my old business showed up unexpectedly.

I asked him what he was doing, and he said he just started another business in the area and that it was taking off and that he was "making a killing." I suddenly felt sorry for myself, I was doing a "woe is me" routine then a voice spoke to me as my friend was still speaking.

The voice asked, "Will you trust Me?" Then with a whimper in my mind I said, "Yes." Then a number flashed in my mind, three hundred but I did not know what it meant. All this was going on while my friend was talking to me in the middle of a bank lobby.

One night as I was in bed with my wife and daughter, I sensed that evil being who used to show up years before to choke me. The same evil, dark, and smirking creature was down the street and just like before, before I knew it, he was right on top of me, even with my family in bed with me.

This time as he started to choke me, I started saying, "In the Name of Jesus Christ I rebuke you" and boom just like that he was gone, he simply disappeared. It was quite a different scenario from years prior. And, he has never returned.

Years before I tried to battle that spirit on my own, but I learned that while we are no match for the war we are facing, the war is no match for God.

Nevertheless, that level of trust I had in God was short lived. As our family was growing, my wife wanted to stay home and homeschool our kids. She homeschooled all of our kids from pre-school through high school. Each of them made the honor roll in junior college before moving to the university with my oldest receiving Summa Cum Laude honors when she graduated.

I thought that I needed to make sure I could provide for our family. Without asking the Lord, I decided to continue my education and thought about going to law school. After all, those guys seemed very successful.

I had a number of high school and college buddies that were very successful attorneys.

Knowing what a terrible student I was, I thought I should first pursue a Master of Business Administration (MBA) degree to help me get the hang of school before I'd go to law school.

Did I pray about it? Did I confirm if it was His will for me? Nope, I made my plans and asked God to confirm it. I still wanted to be in the driver seat, but I was willing to invite God to be in the passenger seat in case I needed His help.

Of course, a school offered a workable finance program and a schedule to fit my work schedule. I thought then that this meant that the Lord was confirming everything. The reality was that I was merely letting favorable circumstances guide me.

Later I learned that if we say we love God, but we allow our circumstances to dictate our responses to our situations, then we might have more faith in our circumstances than in God.

I worked and went to school full time for two-and-a-half years. My plan was to finish up my MBA, go to law school and live happily ever after.

We lived at my parents for almost two years. I had another daughter there as well.

After two years, we moved out of my parents' house and my wife was pregnant again. I was in between jobs at the time, and it was a miracle that we were able to find a place to live while I was unemployed. Shortly after moving into our new place, we found out we were having twins. God sure has a sense of humor, I thought.

One night I could not sleep, and I felt really down. I called the 700 Club early in the morning and cried. The person asked if I had been baptized in the Holy Spirit. I said no, I never heard of baptism in the Holy Spirit, and he said he would send me some material.

I read the material and prayed to be baptized with the Holy Spirit. I was so energized, one night my wife said she saw me sleeping with both my arms up in the air.

We moved to Costa Mesa after moving out of my parents' house and were just a few miles from Calvary Chapel Costa Mesa. This was the same church where I started my spiritual journey years before.

I went to church as much as I could while working on my MBA. When I finally graduated, I made plans for law school. I thought I would get a Chartered Financial Analyst (CFA) designation while going there.

It consisted of one test a year over three years. However, if you failed you had to wait until the following year to retake it.

Again, I pursued it while not confirming anything with the Lord. I even completed my Series 7 during that time, and I became a full-fledged stockbroker.

Now, what were the results of all this activity? Well, I could not get a job with my new MBA, I was overqualified. Plus, I failed the first CFA exam after over 100 hours of studying and my wife put the kibosh on law school. We also had twins coming, and she did not want me to do full time work while going to law school part time.

She went back to work, and I ended up staying home and homeschooling my two girls. One day we were in the pool at our condo and I was watching the gardeners working hard around us.

I told to the Lord that I would not mind working as a gardener. The Lord told me though to stay home and spend time with my kids.

I also made a habit of listening to a number of pastors on the radio. I'd write down what I learned in a notebook and I would read the Bible every day.

That year we somehow ended up saving over $10,000 with just my wife working. In addition, homeschooling and spending time with my girls was actually fun. I taught my second daughter to read, even though this was no easy task (it took lots of Apple Jacks and malt balls to eventually get her to read). I will always relish that time with her.

I was the only dad who showed up for my oldest daughter's girl scout events and meetings. I taught her troop how to play football. We still talk about those days.

Yet my inner man was saying I was a loser, so I tried to talk myself into not enjoying my time with my girls.

During that time however I learned that scripture reveals a God who isn't concerned with your success but is more concerned with your sanctification and how your failures can be used to mold you into His image.

Then our twins were born, and I went back to work while my wife stayed home. We had a boy and a girl, and we had to move again since the place we were renting was sold. We could not find a place in our area. The only place available was in San Juan Capistrano, California and we moved there in 1994.

Those years leading up to our next big move were difficult, but I learned so much, and while I was drawing closer to the truth, I still had many things to learn. Still, I was determined to know truth and was going to seek after it with all that I had.

Chapter 10:
Leaning on God

My first priority was to find a church which taught the Bible verse by verse. I was not interested in its programs or the type of people who went there. Thankfully the Lord opened up a door.

I found a new growing church which taught verse by verse and most of the people there had young children like us. My family got involved and everyone was growing in the Word and after many years we are still friends with many of them even after church splits and people moving away.

As a matter of fact, my oldest daughter married the son of one of the families we knew from there. I think she was only eight years old when we first met them, and today they have three children.

Most of the guys in the church went to a men's study on Tuesday nights. It was led by the assistant pastor who was a caring, loving and God-fearing man.

He mentored all of us. He was patient and his love for Jesus was a great example for us.

One night I was coming home after our study and a limo pulled in front of me as it got off the freeway. I immediately recognized its personalized license plate. It was one of my former associates from when I had my business years before.

He lived in the area and became very successful and went to work in his own chauffeured limo. He also wore custom clothes and smoked cigars in his eight thousand square foot home complete with his own par three golf course.

My mind started to wander after I saw his limo. I thought about what could have been as my Mitsubishi van let out a belch.

Then the Lord assured me that I was in a better place than my old friend was that night. I had to ask myself what I was chasing after. Was I chasing after God's approval or man's approval? Could God trust that I wouldn't turn His gifts to me into idols?

After a few years of going to the men's study, our assistant pastor asked if I wanted to teach one of the studies. I could not believe how excited I was. Never in my wildest imagination could I have imagined that I would be teaching a Bible study and believe me I have a wild imagination.

I have come to believe that teaching or leading a Bible study is one of the greatest honors that can be bestowed on someone. God somehow gives us wretched, poor, weak sinners the opportunity to share His Word with others. It is an amazing honor and one that must be taken seriously should you find yourself in a position to teach and lead in the church.

I also learned that the teacher is more blessed than the attendees because your knowledge of the Bible grows in a special way that can only benefit you.

However, it is still a two-way street, because I have found that most times, God wants us to experience what we are teaching. The truth is how can one talk about trusting God when you have not experienced trusting Him?

James talks about us walking the talk. For example, how can one teach on faith in God when you have never had any faith in Him? I have learned that having a good relationship with God means that we experience Him in our lives.

It is not some detached relationship; it is an active fluid relationship we experience in walking with the Lord. Later I learned that God doesn't call the qualified, instead He qualifies those who are called. God using us has nothing to do with our qualifications, and a Christian devoid of the Word of God will easily fall prey to the devil.

Initially I thought the best way for me to serve God was working with children. After a few years, I led our children's ministry and the AWANA club at our church. In one of the classes I taught, there was a kid who deliberately disturbed the class week after week.

So, I met with his parents and told them I did not want him in my class for one month. It was a good thing they did not tell my pastor or leave the church.

There were lots of incidents of boys just being out of control, bored, not listening or not participating. After a while I realized that working with children was not my calling. I needed more patience.

It was not all challenges though, there were so many great kids, today, some are attorneys, businesspeople, accountants, and more. In addition, the out of control kids are probably pastors somewhere today. God is so good!

In a way, I'm jealous of kids who are exposed to Jesus at such an early age. They won't have to go through a lot of the stupid stuff people like myself have had to go through. They won't have to waste years of their lives like I have.

I found I was enjoying teaching the men's study and was asked to lead more studies. I found that my experience and my walk up to that point was relatable to what some of the guys were going through. In a sense we were learning the Bible together.

God wants you to grow spiritually because when you do, your life becomes more meaningful and more satisfying. People around you will benefit from your spiritual growth.

Eventually, I was invited to join a men's ministry called Combined Men's. My friend who started it asked if I could help out. The focus was to provide a venue for the smaller churches in our area to grow their men's groups.

We had a breakfast once a month in a nice restaurant, and we provided a worship band and had a "big" Christian speaker come in. There was no talk about come and join our church. It was just a blessing to see guys from different churches work together, pray together, and worship together.

The band was made up of guys from different churches. It's sad within the Christian community, sometimes people will just hang with people from their church and only listen to their pastor. As if everyone else has spiritual cooties and their church is the only way to know and grow in Jesus Christ.

A few times there was a mix up with our speakers so we would have the guys come up and speak about what God was doing in their lives. Those times were very powerful. I think men need a place where they can be themselves without having to perform. A place where we can just let everything down and be vulnerable.

When men are going through something, we tend to isolate ourselves and the devil is like a roaring lion, looking for who he can devour. He preys on us when we are alone.

I picture guys who isolate themselves as stragglers in those large herds in Africa. The devil is the lion looking for the weakest ones in the herd. The easy pickings. The devil is looking for the spiritually weak and guys who are alone are easy pickings for him.

We had guys come a hundred miles because they felt they needed to be around some brothers, it was great.

One of our speakers would sometimes prophesy over individuals after his messages. Everyone was scared when he walked around looking intently at each person. Everyone would try to avoid his gaze. If he prophesied over someone; their eyes would become as big as saucers.

He prophesied over me, and I still have it and carry it around in my wallet. We recorded all of our speakers; I was able to write down his prophecy over me. I pull it out once a year or so and wonder if it is true. This is what it was:

The Lord is going to call you out of the back row. You are never one to take the honored place. You are always willing to take the servant's place, the place in the back row. Even as it is revealed in my Word, I say to you, come sit at the table. I've given you gifts, abilities. I've given you vision, now I'm giving you a voice, so fear not, it will not account as your ego doing this.

They will know it is my own Spirit drawing you now, for you have known for a season now is the time to step up to the plate and to do what I've called you to do. You will know you've taken the right path and you've sat in that last seat. Now, I say to you, come to the banqueting table, for I want to pour out in you and through you My blessing and let My joy fill your heart and know that it will not corrupt you and it will not destroy you, because it is My hand that will bring you forth.

I do not know who or how, but we decided to start a Bible study at a local coffee shop over fifteen years ago, and it is still going on today.

The idea is that anyone can come, it doesn't matter what church, and there are no church promotions. I don't consider myself a pastor, I consider myself a facilitator. Guys are encouraged to participate, ask questions and be involved.

All I do is prepare the Bible studies, which are verse by verse. You don't need to be big, eloquent, smart, or famous. God loves you and that is enough! If you are in Christ, you are loved! God knows you and protects you.

For a few years, when my work schedule would not allow, a few guys kept the Bible study going. They told me they knew I would come back sooner or later (they knew my work history!).

My work history since I trusted Jesus instead of myself many years ago has been up and down. I have gone through layoffs and long periods of unemployment. All this uncertainty has caused me to trust in God rather than myself, my degrees, experience or contacts.

Over time I started to see that our real need is spiritual, for our spirit is eternal. I have gone from janitorial work to being a vice president of the largest company in its industry within a three-year period.

Once when I was working for a friend in his janitorial business, he came to pick me up in his two-seater with a hatchback in the back where he kept his buckets and mops.

We had a number of jobs that afternoon. He said he had to pick up his best worker to help with the jobs. We got to his employee's house, and because he only had two seats, I volunteered to lay in the back of the car.

After all, I was not going to let my friend's best worker lay in the back. I was the rookie after all. So, driving from job to job, I would roll around the back trying to keep the wet mops and buckets away from me.

As we were driving back after finishing our jobs, it was dark, and I remember looking up and talking to God. I told Him that I guessed this is where I'd end up, after wanting to conquer the world there I was, mops hitting my face and all.

Shortly after that I was hired by a company in the mortgage industry. After a few months with that company I moved into a national role as a National Business Development Director for a very large company in the industry.

I had the whole US as a territory. My role was working with large banks and credit unions, typically dealing with folks at the VP level. I did a lot of traveling. One week I was in Chicago, New Hampshire and Shreveport. After landing in Shreveport, I remember the guy at the car rental agency asked where I have been that week, I honestly could not remember. I did try to be sure I was home on Fridays to lead the Bible study though.

Three years later, I was a vice president of Strategic Alliances for one of the largest mortgage companies in the world at the time.

I was in charge of building new profitable business channels. The company would come to me and ask how to grow their business in a particular channel or segment. I would then write business plans and submit them to the company.

They would review them and say yes or no. If it was a yes, I would launch it, hire a person to manage it for six figures and act as a consultant for the business channel.

They actually said yes to all of my business plans. The company gave me access to all of the resources I needed too.

There was no budget, as long as I made money. One of the new business channels I started generated over three billion in new business for the company the second year. The president made that channel a top three initiative for the company at the end of the year.

I ended up developing five new business channels. I was included in all meetings involving business development. I took all calls regarding new partnerships as well.

Once I was in a meeting with a new Seattle based start-up in the real estate business. The founder was there, he had a dot-com company which he sold for millions and was launching a new start-up and wanted to partner with us.

We turned him down and today his company is doing very well. However, my former company is gone.

Once an internal information technology (IT) person called and asked how I was coming up with all my ideas and strategies. I told her I had an MBA, a Six Sigma Black Belt (a process improvement certification), and that I had my own businesses and was well read on business strategies.

After I hung up, it was as if the Lord tapped me on the shoulder and said, "Ah, excuse Me!" So, I called her back up, set up a meeting the next day and talked to her about my reading the Bible, knowing Jesus as my Savior and I told how her apart from Him I could do nothing.

Isn't it so easy for us to dictate to God how He can and cannot glorify Himself in our lives?

I find it interesting when I was getting recognized within a large company and bringing in business, and people wanting to transfer to my group.

Yet, there were people who were actually mad at me for whatever reason. I realized there were always company and office politics going on. I usually avoided going out with my co-workers for lunch because I had too much work.

I also avoided cognac and cigars after work because I had to catch the train home.

I think that all of my excuses eventually worked against me. When you have people, there will always be some kind of politics going on. I once worked for a start-up, there were only three of us on staff and there were still politics going on.

Whenever I had a good job, we learned not to change our lifestyle or accumulate debt because my work history made us realize that things always seemed like they would be short-lived. We had to learn to live on a budget and not pay retail for stuff.

During long periods of unemployment, I made sure to spend my time looking for work. When I was unemployed, my job was always looking for a job. I usually spent eight hours or so a day looking for work.

I learned a couple of other things too during those times. God's faithfulness to His children depends on His righteousness, not on ours. The fulfillment of His promises will come according to His plan, not ours.

He uses our circumstances to deepen our relationship with Him. The one who created you ultimately knows what will truly satisfy your soul, even better than you do. Both lessons were and still are very hard for me to learn.

One time we went to Yosemite for a vacation, and I found an area that had free Wi-Fi. I took my laptop, got on my bike and looked for work while vacationing there.

I kept hearing about that verse, that says that he who doesn't provide for his family is worse than an infidel.

Yet I also kept thinking back to that time in the bank when God asked me if I would trust Him and I said yes. I thought about how everything I was going through related to the chapter on faith in 1 Corinthians 13.

People go through stuff so God can test their faith in Him. How else are we to learn if His promises to us are true or not?

Look at the Apostle Paul and all the other Apostles went through for that matter. Of course, Jesus Christ's sacrifice appears as foolishness to those who don't know Him.

As 2 Corinthians 1:18 states, "For the message of the cross is foolishness to those who are perishing, but to us who are being saved it is the power of God."

The Apostles were all in God's will, yet they still experienced trials. Various other thoughts went through my mind during my time in the mountains on that trip.

Are we supposed to trust God only when things are going well? Are we too busy trying to create heaven on earth? Am I working for man's approval or God's?

I felt people were trying to stay away from me, like I had some bad juju on me. I felt people were not accepting me because I was a failure, even in my own family.

What about resting on the Lord? Was is it my fault that I could not land a new job? These thoughts continued until one day, while I was in the middle of combing the internet and sending out resumes, I was discouraged and asked God why this was happening to me.

I felt the Lord ask me, "Why are you kicking against the goads?" I had to ask myself three things that I believe we all need to ask during certain seasons in our life. They are:

- Am I in this situation because of sin or pride?
- Do I believe I am in God's will?
- If I could answer no to the first question and yes to the second, then I must be in God's will and then that meant that I was in the best place I could be.

I was caught up in believing that failure was a person and that that person was me. Through all these years I have learned that failure is an event, not a person, and that our trials are an opportunity to trust in the Lord.

I told my wife I was going to take a break from looking for work. She panicked and told our pastor that I had given up. A few months later I got a new job from a resume I sent in months before.

God was taking care of us through those years and He continues to do so today. I have had to keep remembering back to that time I said I would trust Him.

As Proverbs 3:5-6 states, "Trust in the Lord with all your heart and lean not on your own understanding: In all your ways acknowledge Him and He shall direct your paths."

Chapter 11:
Who God Says We Are

One time, we had a good friend of ours who had a Christmas ministry. She would transform into Mrs. Clause and would go around and bless families in need.

Around October one year she asked if my family would like to be the family that she would bless that year. I had been unemployed for a long while at that point and we were without insurance. I said ok, even though my pride had always made it hard for me to accept charity.

I used to tell the kids when we went on our walks and they tried to jump or run too fast, "Careful, we don't have insurance."

I've always easily allowed my mind to berate me and tell me that I'm such a poor provider and that I'm worse than an infidel.

She asked if I would ask the kids what they wanted. I asked my family and gave Mrs. Clause the list and forgot about it. Around early December I decided to go play basketball to relive my past and forget about my present.

As I made a move to do a one-handed slam (in my dreams!) with no one guarding me, I heard a pop. It felt like someone hit the back of my foot with a baseball bat.

I called foul, but the guys said there was no one around me. I limped off the court wondering what happened.

Later I learned I ruptured my Achilles tendon. Of course, we had no insurance and Christmas was fast approaching. I was planning to put up Christmas lights and get a Christmas tree that day and I had no money for presents.

I got an unexpected call from Mrs. Clause asking when she could come by with the kids' presents. I had actually forgotten about her and I told her what happened.

She called someone to drop a tree off and the next day, three vans showed up loaded with presents. The floor of the living room was filled with presents. I could not have afforded all them even if I had a job.

There were gift cards to various grocery stores too. We had so much that I was able to give some of it to others in need too.

As for my Achilles tendon, I was able to have an appointment with one of the top orthopedic surgeons in the area. I remember he had a couple of med students with him talking about how I had a classic rupture.

Then he casually asked me, "By the way, who do you have your insurance with?" I was honest and said that I didn't have insurance. The room emptied so fast; I was left alone hearing crickets. I actually had to show myself out.

To make a long story short, that same surgeon volunteered to do my surgery later along with his support staff. It cost me my last $800 which I believe they didn't even receive. It just went to the state.

The surgery was done just in time. I learned that if a certain amount of time passes; the Achilles tendon rolls up and is harder to attach. I was so blessed to have the procedure done when it was and I'm forever grateful to God for working it all out.

We always have to remember that we live to play a role in God's story, not He is ours. It's all about Him, not about us. He is central, we are peripheral.

If the kids had a request or something in mind, I would ask them if they ever asked God first or prayed about it before coming to ask me. Was it because I was super holy? No, it was because I didn't have the resources to help them.

I made a point of thanking Jesus for any blessing we received. A little while ago, I heard my oldest daughter thanking Jesus for something simple that happened. It blessed me so much.

I wanted to surrender everything to God, including their needs and wants because I was not in a position to give things to them for most of their lives.

It was very tough on my ego but, I had to rely on God's mercy and grace. Don't miss the opportunity to allow God to use your failures for His glory and for the good of others.

Over the years I developed the practice of getting up early in the morning before going surfing and praying in the living room on my knees while everyone was sleeping. I did this for years. However, today I can't do it anymore since my knees hurt.

There were times when my kids would wake up early and see me. At times I felt that was the only thing I could do. I used to pride myself on being independent. I believed I could do anything I set my mind on.

I then realized that way was leading me to eternal death. I had to be totally God dependent, not self-reliant. I wanted my family to see their dad on his knees praying to God so that it would help them see how much I depended and relied on the Lord.

As I mentioned, God was taking care of us in supernatural ways. There were times when I found anonymous envelopes with money in them in my mailbox. A few times friends found money and said God told them to give it to me.

I have found boxes of food in the front of the house. Once, I was sent a check from an old company I was with. I didn't know but I was part of a class action suit against the company. The money was just enough to cover our rent for that month.

I was also learning to ask myself if I wanted more *of* God or more *from* God? More from God meant using Him to accomplish my goals. It meant just seeking Him to get what I wanted. I learned to want more of God and not more from Him.

I remember when my oldest daughter wanted to get married and move to Hawaii to go to school.

She always wanted to go to college in Hawaii, even as a young girl. I had maybe $300 at the time and she wanted a big wedding with over three hundred and fifty or so in attendance. Basically, that amounted to everyone at our church plus all of our relatives.

Talk about feeling like a total loser, yet God stepped in. Everyone pitched in and volunteered. It was a wonderful wedding and I still had the $300 after it was all over. Today, my daughter and her family live in Maui with three beautiful girls of their own.

When my second oldest daughter got married, I found myself in a similar situation. We had less people, maybe only seventy-five but God took care of everything. It too was nothing short of miraculous.

All four of my kids went to junior college and three of them graduated from the university. They all had to work and pay their way through school. It was tough when my youngest was going to school at the University of Hawaii (both my oldest and youngest graduated from there), knowing she did not have a car and had to either ride the bus or walk a long distance to go to church.

I think in the long-term these things benefitted them. They learned to be independent, what it is to struggle and to trust God for their needs. There's a non-Christian proverb that I just recently learned. This is a paraphrase and it goes something like this, "One does not know the value of a drop of water unless he carries the bucket from the river."

Maybe only people from a third world country will understand that. A great blessing was that college did not negatively influence their love and dependence for the Lord in the slightest.

My oldest daughter received a full ride academic scholarship. She even gave the graduation speech when she graduated from the University of Hawaii with her bachelor's in accounting.

She told us the morning of her graduation that she was giving the graduation speech and we were so happy. She gave God all the glory.

I always used to pray Colossians 3:23 to my kids, which states "In all that you do, do it heartily unto the Lord." She quoted that very verse in her graduation speech, and to a secular audience no less!

I tried to encourage my kids to look to the Lord and not to me. Maybe it's a cop out from a worldly perspective, I know. But I wanted them to rely on God and not me because I knew I would disappoint them.

I know God loves them more than I could ever love them and that He cares for them more than I could ever care for them.

My love for them at best is occasionally an agape love, and most of the time it is a familial love, yet God's love for them is unconditional all the time. I wanted them to build their own Ebenezer stones, to build their own relationship and dependence on God.

When Joshua was leading the Israelites to the Promised Land, God asked Joshua to put stones down where God did miracles for them so that when their kids would ask them what the stones where there for, they could tell them about what God did for them.

God told Joshua to call those stones, Ebenezer stones. In them the Israelites had a visual remembrance of God's deliverance through the wilderness.

I wanted my kids to remember God's working in their lives at an early age, to develop their own "Ebenezer" stones, their own faith in God and not in me. Because whether or not you receive His comfort depends on how deeply you trust His character and how surrendered you are to His will.

In hindsight, it was the best thing I could ever have done. In the moment however I often thought and called myself the world's greatest loser. "Here's the worlds' biggest loser trying to find a job, going surfing, going to church, eating breakfast, and so on" was my thought process more times than not.

One day I was driving and calling myself the world's biggest loser when a big pebble hit the window of my van right on the driver's side. It snapped me out of it, and I stopped the negative talk.

I think that pebble was meant to harm me and possibly take my life and somehow it did not cause me any harm, though it did leave a nice big crack on the wind shield.

Anyway, I started to replace all the negative thoughts I was having with God's promises that He has for us in the Bible. The following verses in particular made such a difference for me:

- "I will never leave you or forsake you." (Heb. 13:5)
- "Yes, I have loved you with an everlasting love: therefore, with lovingkindness I have drawn you." (Jer. 31:3)
- "For as the heavens are higher than the earth, so are My ways higher than your ways, And My thoughts than your thoughts." (Is. 55:9)
- "For I know the thoughts that I think toward you, says the Lord, thoughts of peace and not evil, to give you a future and a hope." (Jer. 29:11)
- "And we know all things work together for good to those who are called according to His purpose." (Rom. 8:28)
- "And whatever you do, do it heartily, as to the Lord and not to men." (Col. 3:23)
- "Casting all your cares upon Him, for He cares for you." (1 Pet. 5:7)

- "Let us therefore come boldly to the throne of grace, that we may obtain mercy and find grace to help in time of need." (Heb. 4:16)
- "Finally, brethren, whatever thigs are true, whatever things are noble, whatever things are just, whatever things are pure, whatever things are lovely, whatever things are of good report, if there is any virtue and if there is anything praiseworthy-meditate on these things." (Phil. 4:8)

And one of my favorites is 1 John 3:1 which states, "Behold what manner of love the Father has bestowed upon us, that we should be called children of God!"

Even after my wife stated she didn't like me or want to be with me years ago, these verses have been very assuring. We have been able to remain married by God's grace.

Even without her acceptance of me and my failures, the Lord continued to promise me that He loves and accepts me. We are not what we have done or what we struggle with, we are who God says we are.

Below are some statements from various devotionals that also have provided me with great comfort and have helped me from going further down a bad road:

- Faith thrives in discomfort. Trust in God's ability and not your feelings. Nothing great happens in your comfort zone.

- We are not what we fear. We are who God says we are.
- God is greater than my failures, fears, limitations, circumstances, obstacles, needs, and my expectations.
- God holds my very breath in His Hand, when He opens His Hand, He alone can satisfy me, sustain me and provide me with the security I need.

Chapter 12: Vignettes

My son recently experienced the Lord's deliverance. He and four of his roommates moved out of their dorms into an old refurbished home in San Diego about two blocks from the beach in Ocean Beach.

They have a nice sweeping ocean view and all of the kids attend Point Loma University, a Christian college in San Diego. All of them are Christians.

I asked my son how things have been going in his new place, and he said strange things were happening in their new house.

For instance, one day he told me that he saw two shoe prints on the middle of the carpet in his bedroom. They appeared as if someone was putting weight on them. He said it was as if someone was standing there but there were no shoeprints on the carpet leading up to the where they were.

As it turned out, he found out that the previous owner died in his room. My son said lights were flickering, doors were swinging open, and even the backyard gate would open and close.

He said there was a strange feeling that someone was in the house and there was such a feeling of dread that no one wanted to stay there.

I remembered back to the time years ago when that evil creature would come visit me. My son grew up in the church and had accepted Jesus Christ as His Lord and Savior when he was younger.

I reminded my son, greater is He who is in you then he who is in the world. I told him that he should rebuke whatever it was in the name of Jesus Christ.

A week later I asked him how things were in the new house. He said his room was fine, but the rest of the house was pretty bad. He had to sleep on the floor in his roommates' room because of all the activity going on in the room was freaking them out.

I asked if he rebuked whatever spirit was there throughout the house. He said just in his room. I told him he had to go to every room including the backyard with his roommates and rebuke it in the name of Jesus Christ.

As it turned out everyone else chickened out. So, my 22-year old son had to go throughout the house and backyard by himself, and rebuke whatever was there in the name of Jesus Christ.

Today, their house is at peace because of God's promise in 1 John 4:4 which states, "You are of God, little children, and have overcome them, because He who is in you is greater than he who is in the world."

In the end we are no match for the war we are facing. Yet the war is also no match for God! We can't do God's work without God's power.

Over the years as I've led Bible studies in public places, it's been interesting to see how many people come and go.

One of our guys was able to help a homeless person who used to sit on a bench by a coffee shop in San Juan Capistrano where we met. He would still be drunk at 7:00 a.m. He would have trash all around him, and his pants would be wet from urinating on himself practically every morning.

One week, one of our guys invited him to stay at his house. The guy wound up getting cleaned up and he was baptized at church and the next week he was at our Bible study. I'll never forget seeing him at the coffee shop that morning, he had showered, was sober, and had gotten haircut. He also had a Bible with him. I almost didn't recognize him!

After that week, he was back on the streets. It wasn't even two weeks later, and there he was pushing a cart, drunk, and smiling a drunk's smile as if nothing had ever happened.

To make a long story short, we were actually able to get him help. He eventually became sober, and he has been off the streets for over ten years. In fact, the last thing I heard was that he was complaining about gaining weight due to the good food he was finally eating! It's a wonderful story though of God's care.

One time a young man showed up at the Bible study. He was probably nineteen years old. He said he was a streetfighter and that he never backed down from any fights and I believed him.

He accepted the Lord as his Savior, and the next week he showed up and told us all that he had written a song about Jesus and he asked if he could play it. How could we possibly refuse?

Right there in the coffee shop, he took out his guitar and started singing a beautiful love song he wrote to God. I almost cried.

He showed up another time with some welts on his face. He said he got in a fight, and that he kind of let the guy beat on him. He said his friends wanted to look for the guy, and that while he knew who he was he didn't tell his friends.

He was through with his street fighting life. He then got a job, a girlfriend and started going to church, though we did not hear from him for a while. He then showed up with his dad months later, and he led his dad to the Lord. Even though we have not heard from him since, I have a feeling he is doing just fine.

Another person showed up one summer, he was very knowledgeable about the Bible. He was a fairly big guy and very humble.

After that summer he said he had to go back home to Dallas. He had a place on the beach in San Clemente, CA and spent the summers there. I remember him sharing how his old football coach; Tom Landry was instrumental in the growth of his faith.

We could not believe it! He was a former middle linebacker for the Cowboys, and was All-Pro, and had been to the Super Bowl three or four times. I remember watching him on TV in the 70s.

He played with Roger Staubach. He was so humble and low key. He ran the men's ministry for his mega-church.

He has been coming back every summer since then. Once, he had a guy with him which was not unusual, he would usually bring friends who were staying with him at the beach house. The following week, he said that the person was his pastor from his mega-church in Dallas.

Another time, a person just came in and sat in the middle of our study and didn't say a word. We kept on with our study, and afterwards we started talking with him. He said he was a former Satanist and that he wrote a book called *Ascent from Darkness* which was in process of becoming a movie called *The Adversary*.

He told us that he would stay with some friends in San Juan Capistrano when he would have meetings in Hollywood. He even rode his Harley all the way from Oklahoma City to California. He's become a good friend ever since. In fact, he was the last person I saw and spoke with prior to my heart attack.

Another time, a week after my mom died, there was a lady we had never seen before sitting on the couch where we do our study.

We were surprised to find someone sitting on "our" seats at the coffee shop when we were supposed to be doing our Bible study. We kindly told her we were going to start a Bible study.

Usually people run away when you start laying your Bibles down on tables. She said it wasn't a problem at all and she encouraged us to do our study. She didn't mind at all.

She actually sat quietly and listened. After we got done, we were talking about my mother's passing that week. She asked if she could pray for my mom. She said she was Jewish, and she would like to get some stuff from her car.

She came back with her Torah and a prayer shawl. She stood up in the middle of the coffee shop, put on her shawl, opened up her Torah and prayed for my mom in Hebrew. I think that was a gift from God.

Some of the same guys would sit around us listening without committing to being in a Bible study, one of them would even pretend to be reading a newspaper.

He would put his paper down; ask a question and go back to reading after getting his question answered. This person claimed to be an event crasher. He said he would take the train to Los Angeles with his bike, lock up his bike and sneak into events dressed in jeans and tuxedo shirts and jackets.

The person was homeless and didn't do any drugs or drink alcohol. He was well spoken, and never asked for charity and he was very clean. He was simply homeless by choice. He had family living inland but he chose to be homeless so he could be by the beach, Laguna Beach in particular.

He spoke about all of the events he had crashed through the years, the Emmys, the Academy Awards, any big event you could think of in LA. I was skeptical however the next week he showed up with hundreds of pictures of himself with every celebrity you could think of.

He had them separated into old and new albums. The old album included pictures of him with Elizabeth Taylor and Michael Jackson. The new one had pictures of him with Lady Gaga wearing her meat dress.

There were not just pictures of celebrities, he was in all of the photos. For a homeless person, he's had movies and newspaper articles talk about his life.

He had become so well known that security groups routinely kept their eyes out for him at events. I asked him what he would tell celebrities when he would meet them. He said he told them he was in sales.

To this day you can find him in Laguna Beach in the summers where he is considered the unofficial greeter for the area, among his other endeavors.

Laguna Beach had an event honoring their greeters recently and of course he was honored. He said once he was sitting at the Academy Awards and the whole row he was sitting in stood up to receive an award but he thought it would look suspicious if he stayed seated while the whole row went on the stage, so he got up with the group and went on stage with them.

His family was watching the show and his kids asked his wife, what's dad doing on stage at the Academy Awards? I'm telling you I couldn't make this stuff up if I tried! He even had a picture of an actress who just won an Emmy and he was holding her Emmy in the picture.

He sat and listened to us and asked questions. He had a few years' worth of the Bible in him. I believe our lives are not accidental, that we're here for a reason. What you do matters to God, even the everyday small stuff.

We also have had people yell at us and have had other groups give us the stink eye. A few times, some would bang on the window of the coffee shop and give us the Italian salute.

Some store managers would have the music very loud when we would come in. When we would ask them to kindly turn down the volume, they would tell us that the volume is controlled in headquarters, and they could not adjust the volume in the store. We all knew that was not true.

Hell appears as God's gesture of support for human choice. All receive what they actually choose. Hell is the end of a long road of choices in living without God. Hell is the result of God lovingly not forcing us to choose to follow Him. Our choices on earth determine where we spend eternity.

Since 2001 I have been giving and leaving Bible tracts everywhere, I go.

As Isaiah 55:11 states, "So shall my word be that goes forth from My mouth; it shall not return to me void, but it shall accomplish what I please. And it shall prosper in the thing which I sent it."

There is a person who walks around town wearing headphones and she has regular conversations to whatever voice she hears on her headphones.

Once I heard her say, "I'm ready for the day." She followed me around that day which I thought odd, but it was apparently because she found one of my Bible tracts.

She walked up to the window while we were doing the Bible study and she tore the tract up in front of us with a smirk on her face. She knows my schedule and she still goes to the areas where she knows I will be on a given day.

I have had jobs that covered anywhere from the western states, to the whole country and that have even included international locations. I have had the opportunity to drop off tracts all over the country.

Since 2001, there have been only two other times when I have personally seen Bible tracts left by others. Once I was in Saskatoon, Saskatchewan for a meeting. I went out to my car one morning from the hotel and saw that someone woke up early and put Bible tracts on all the cars in the parking lot. It was very encouraging.

Another time, an old friend handed me a tract, the same tract I was dropping off, and I thought he picked up one of my tracts and was giving it back to me. Turns out, he was passing out the same tracts himself.

People who know that I drop off tracts usually ask me if I was at a certain store or at the beach because they saw one of my tracts there. The best places to drop tracts off are airport waiting areas by the way.

I told the Lord, even if I don't have the funds, I will continue to purchase and drop off Bible tracts. My desire is to share the good news and the results are up to the Holy Spirit. Today, my eight and three-year-old grandsons often ask me if they can have some tracts to pass out. It warms my heart.

Today, I'm leading a few more Bible studies and I look forward to God continuing to lead people to our little studies. The secret to leading a Bible study is to find a public place, like a coffee shop and use a Bible, not your phone.

Also, you need to make sure you are prayed up and trusting Him. Our studies are very casual. We act normal, not stuffy and there are never stoic looks on our faces. I have learned with men; homework is not a good idea. We go verse by verse.

The Bible says that we are a peculiar people. I always tell people in Bible studies to forget about being politically correct. I tell them to be themselves.

You don't have to speak in King James English or act like you know everything. I noticed guys will lower their voices a few octaves when talking about the Bible, maybe they think it makes them sound more holy. I have not heard anyone come in speaking in a loud Southern accent yet, maybe someday. Don't take things personally, people will disagree with you, be mean, insult you, and challenge you. You just have to roll with it and remember that we are just messengers.

I have to remind myself about all the times I rejected people who tried to reach out to me with the Good News. We are just spokes in the wheel of that person's life that God is using to lead them closer to Him. Nevertheless, we do have to love God's people and we must also rely on the Holy Spirit at all times.

After all of these years of leading Bible studies and watching God work in my life, I still struggle with so many things. I still have a lot of bad habits which carry over from my days without Jesus. A few of the issues are driving, crowds and waiting in long lines.

- **Driving:** I could be in the car, with the windows rolled up listening to a great Christian song on the radio. I can be singing and feeling it and suddenly someone cuts me off, I will freak. Suddenly in my mind, I'm breaking two to three of the Ten Commandments! Then I realize what I'm doing and ask God for forgiveness.

Sometimes, I would try to catch up to the person and see who would drive like that and often I'd notice that the person is oblivious to everything and doesn't even know that they almost killed me.

Today, I try to think that the reason they are driving crazy is maybe because they are having an emergency and are headed to a hospital. I try to remember to pray for their safety. Thank God for 1 John 1:9 which states that, "If we confess our sins, He is faithful and just to forgive us our sins and cleanse us from all unrighteousness."

Crowds: My family knows how I try to avoid crowds at all costs. Long lines-especially at stores like Costco really bother me.

I always spend time analyzing and scoping out the shortest line, then I rush over to it and will run over children if I have too just to save a few seconds.

I'll pat myself on the back once in line only to see the person pull out coupons, have issues with their card or a shift change. Once, I saw the person in front of me with a loaded cart say to the cashier that he forgot his credit card, I don't know how he got in. I made the comment to the lady behind me, "I always get stuck in these kind of lines" and she said, "So do I, that's why I'm stuck behind you." I'll then watch other people in the other lines getting out before me and it drives be bonkers.

Of course, the worst is a combination of crowds and long lines. Like trying to get out of the church parking lot. My kids when they were younger would remind me that it's not a good idea to honk your horn in the church parking lot, especially at the pastor's car!

Regardless of all these things I'm working on becoming more patient. Maybe God has me waiting in line to avoid an accident outside or because He wants me to use my time to speak to someone about Him rather than complaining about always being stuck in the wrong line.

2 Peter 3:9 states, "The Lord is not slack concerning His promise, as some count slackness, but is longsuffering toward us, not willing that any should perish but that all should come to repentance."

Knowing God is longsuffering towards me has always been a great comfort to me.

Something I still struggle with after all these years is that I'm still easily intimidated by others in our Bible studies. I never went to seminary. I'm not a Bible expert. Some of the guys that come to our studies are former missionaries, Christian business leaders and pastors.

I just continue to surrender the studies to Him. I pray that He alone gets the glory and for Him to put the words in my mouth that He wants me to say.

I just make sure I'm available and in hindsight I can see how God has continued to use my past failures and disappointments to relate to the guys. As I said at the beginning and throughout this book, in spite of me, He loves me. He is in control and I can trust Him.

Chapter 13:
What It's All About

Remembering the vision, I had during my heart attack season always brings me great comfort. Thinking about the great peace, love and acceptance I experienced during that brief time has helped assure me that He is for me, not against me.

I've learned a lot by looking back on my life and thinking about all of the identities and failures I experienced outside of Jesus Christ. My life has been like an onion and as I peel off the various identities that I tried to create through the different stages of my life, my identity as a father, husband, skier, surfer, business person, employee, employer, I've realized that at the very core I was always just a sinner in desperate need of a Redeemer and a Savior.

I was building a house of cards. My house was built on a foundation of pride, self-centeredness and independence from God.

I had to replace that foundation, I had to be born again and replace that independent, prideful and sin laden foundation with Jesus Christ for He alone is the author and finisher of my faith.

The change that needed to happen was from the inside out, not the outside in. Laying all those layers on top of my sinful foundation to hide it might have fooled people and given me some worldly things as a result, but all that in the end would just have been temporary.

In the light of eternity, the most meaningful change I needed to make was to replace my sinful foundation with a foundation built on the "Rock," Jesus Christ. My identity had to be in Jesus Christ alone, and I am forever thankful that now it is.

I've learned that if I live my life for an audience of One, everything else takes care of itself. I don't have to worry about pleasing anyone, but God. With that mindset in place He will take care of everything else.

I don't have to worry about my past or my tomorrow. In fact, He even said not to worry…

"…do not worry about your life, what you will eat or what you will drink, nor about your body, what you will put on. Is not life more than food and the body more than clothing?" (Matt. 6:25)

"Therefore, do not worry about tomorrow, for tomorrow will worry about its own things. Sufficient for the day is its own troubles." (Matt. 6:34)

Here are few other statements about worry that have blessed me:

- Worry happens when we seek the created and not the Creator.
- Ultimately, only God is worthy of fear.
- 85% of situations we worry about don't happen. And of the 15% that do happen, 79% are not as bad as we thought they would be.
- To praise the Lord in the midst of our problems glorifies His name.
- If your heart has followed after God, then God has been leading you and you have been doing His will, perhaps without even knowing it.
- What we stress about reveals what we care about. Stop giving stress power over your life.

I remember through all of our financial challenges opening up the refrigerator door and seeing it full of food. We never missed a meal, borrowed money or used our credit cards to live. We were even living in an area that we liked.

God has always been good to us, in spite of me.

As I was growing closer to the Lord, I became concerned with my parents' salvation. Sure, they went to church and followed all the rules of their religion. But did they have a personal relationship with Jesus Christ?

My mother went through so much from surviving breast cancer, strokes, diabetes and assorted other health issues. One day, my father called and told me my mom was on her last leg. It was so serious that he told me that's she might not make it by the time I got there.

I called the closest Calvary Chapel to the hospital, Calvary Chapel in Cypress. I spoke with a pastor and explained to him the situation about my mom. He said he would go visit her at the hospital right away.

A few hours later I spoke with the pastor and he said my mom accepted Jesus Christ as her Savior! He said my father kept leaving the room whenever he mentioned Jesus. My mom lived for a few more years after that until she passed away peacefully at home at eighty-six years old.

One day my father called and asked me if I knew anyone who could build wheelchair ramps in his house. This was towards the last days of my mom's life when she was confined to a wheelchair.

I didn't know of any construction people in their area, so I called Calvary Chapel Downey. The receptionist said they did not refer people, but that there was a flyer on her desk advertising a handy man.

The flyer had a fish symbol on it. She wondered aloud how the flyer got on her desk since she apparently sat in the very back of the office.

I thought it was from the Lord. She gave me the number, I called it, and the person said he lived close to my parents and that he could go and see my dad that afternoon.

I spoke with him again that afternoon, and he said he led my dad to the Lord. He became close to my dad after my mom died. They would go to Home Depot together often.

My dad told me that he liked him, but that he sure talked too much about God. If I could not get a hold of my dad, I would call the handyman to check on him. He said he looked at my dad like the grandfather he never had, and he would read the Bible to my father a lot.

My father was diagnosed with leukemia at the age of ninety-two. He was put on hospice and passed one month later at home after his diagnosis.

He was constantly praising and thanking Jesus that last month. My father and I were opposites and were never really that close to each other until the last few years of his life.

We would go to lunch and he would open up like he never did before. He talked about growing up in the Philippines during the war, going out by himself at night with his .22 at only fourteen years old and trying to shoot Japanese soldiers.

He said he had seven notches on his gun. He had so many stories, I wish I recorded them. It was as if he knew life was ending and he wanted to get everything out. I'm so glad I was able to spend time with him those last few years.

In spite of my failure to lead them to the Lord, God answered my prayers and He used others to do it. When I pray today, I constantly remind myself who the Lord is, and I want to share with you as well just Who He is…

He is the Creator of heaven and earth. He spoke everything into existence. He created everything seen and unseen. He created everything from nothing. All of the earth and all of its fullness are His.

What's impossible with man is possible with Him. He loves you with an everlasting love and draws you to Him with bands of lovingkindness.

He will never leave you or forsake you. Nothing can separate you form His love. All things work out for good to those who love Him and have been called according to His purpose.

You are His child. He thinks upon you. His thoughts about you are as many as the sand on the seashore. He paid your debt on the cross. A debt you could never ever pay back, a debt He did not owe. His last words on the cross were, "It is finished." I think He meant that He paid the price for our sins. We don't have to knock on so many doors to earn or work our way to heaven.

In John 3:3 Jesus said, "Most assuredly, I say to you, unless one is born again, he cannot see the kingdom of God".

As I start my day today, I pray that I may please and worship the Lord and that His will would be done today and not my will.

For me, praying that His will be done and not my will and really meaning it was and is the hardest prayer for me. Love without freedom is manipulation. God does not manipulate us, He loves us. His sovereign plan includes our choices.

I try to keep the following verses in mind to help me.

- "Be anxious for nothing, but in everything by prayer and supplication, with thanksgiving, let your requests be made known to God: and the peace of God which surpasses all understanding will guard your hearts and minds in Christ Jesus." (Phil. 4:6-7)

- "Rejoice always, pray without ceasing, in everything give thanks; for this is the will of God in Christ Jesus for you." (1 Thess. 3:16-18)

- "Only let your conduct be worthy of the Gospel of Christ…" (Phil. 1:27)

I have learned that our biggest battle is between our ears. Guilt is from the devil; conviction is from the Holy Spirit.

I have to continually saturate my mind with what the Lord wants me to meditate on as Philippians 4:8 teaches.

Did you know that the one who created you ultimately knows what will truly satisfy your soul even better than you do? Spending time with God helps us to get to know Him better. It's worth giving God first place in your life.

With all that I have learned about God's love for me, I still let the circumstances of my life and their worries affect me. I believe the stress I let overcome me led to my heart attack.

Prior to my father's passing, he showed me his trust and I noticed there were changes made after the original trust date. I did not say anything. It was no big deal to me, my parents could change it anyway they wanted, it was their trust after all.

However, he also told me about how he wanted the arrangements for his funeral. He had his suit with a corsage picked out, his coffin, pictures to use, a police escort from the church to the cemetery, a restaurant for the lunch, and more all settled ahead of time.

My father was an engineer; he was very organized. Forest Lawn cemetery was amazed at how organized he was, they said he was the most organized client they ever had!

Shortly after his burial, I set to work on dispersing his assets. While he and my mom were alive, I encouraged them to spend their money and not worry about us.

They had always saved and were able to live the American dream, even with their late start in this country. My dad was always proud of the fact he was able to set aside something for his children. I know they worked extremely hard and sacrificed so much for us, and I wanted so much to honor them with their last wishes.

That's when I started getting comments like, "You never did anything good for mom and dad," and "You don't deserve any money," and of course "When you were 12 years old you tried to fight dad...you didn't even live with us when you were little, you lived with grandma" and also "You moved back in with our parents" and the list goes on.

There was stuff brought up that I forgot about, and I just tried to keep my head down, get my work done and move on. Unfortunately, I let everything affect me, which I believe led to my heart attack.

Still, as Genesis 50:20 states, "But as for you, you meant evil against me, but God meant it for good."

I have forgiven all who have helped cause my heart attack and I have moved on, yet an important question remains. How should I live the rest of my life? What's next? After the Lord shared that incredible vision of His peace, His love and His acceptance of me, in spite of me.

I sometimes feel like I'm in one of those old Disneyland commercials. Disneyland would ask someone right after they won some type of championship, "You just won the Super Bowl, what are you going to do next?" They would answer, "I'm going to Disneyland!"

In my case, "You just spent time in heaven with Jesus Christ, what are you going to do next?"

It's an essential question, especially since this life can go by so quickly. I had no idea I would have a heart attack that afternoon. The odds were stacked against me. My surgeon said it was a 1 in 500,000 chance against me.

I started considering what James says in James 4:14, "whereas you do not know what will happen tomorrow. For what is your life? It is even a vapor that appears for a little time and then vanishes away."

I've also remembered this comment from a devotional I read recently which says that your weakness is your opportunity to trust God. It all depends on whom you have your hope in.

It was very difficult writing this story. It was hard going back through my life and replaying the emotions of all my failures.

Yet God has shown me how He loves and accepts me, all in spite of me. That fact is so very comforting.

As I look at what He has done in my life so far, I can see so many blessings. I'm still alive, still have a roof over my head, am still married, have four successful kids and six beautiful grandchildren with more coming. All I can say is, "Thank you, Lord!"

I know God has a purpose for my life, and that my heart attack was simply a part of that purpose. Maybe most of all it was meant to encourage just one person. Perhaps that one person...is you?

Epilogue:
Answering the Call

Do you feel that you are a square peg in a round world? Are you a person who feels unloved and unaccepted?

God wants you to know that He loves you and accepts you. After all, if He can love and accept someone like me, in spite of me, then he wants to love you just as much.

He wants you to know that He loves you and accepts you, too. In spite of you.

All you have to do is ask Jesus Christ to be the Lord and Savior of your life. As John 3:16-17 states, "For God so loved the world that He gave His only begotten Son, that whoever believes in Him will not perish but have everlasting life. For God did not send His Son into the world to condemn the world, but that the world through Him might be saved."

You know…in spite of me, in spite of you, in spite of what you say about you or what the world says about you, Jesus still accepts you. He accepts you in spite of you.

He loved you when you are the most unlovable. He accepted you even then. There is no quid pro quo with Him.

Still, we must all choose to accept His offer of salvation and forgiveness through His Son, Jesus Christ. We must be born again.

You see there are only two options when it comes to where we will all spend eternity. Heaven or hell. Where you spend eternity rests on who you say Jesus Christ is.

I've often told people about the dash between the dates of someone's birth and death as displayed on gravestones.

The decisions you make in the dash will determine if you will have eternal life or eternal death. The decision is solely yours.

Your race, country, politics, family, church, and friends cannot make the decision for you. You cannot ride anyone's coat tails to heaven. You must make the decision on your own.

Jesus may be knocking on the door of your heart, but you must decide if you will open the door to let Him in or if you will ignore Him.

Once you accept Him, read the Bible. The Bible is our roadmap for life. As 2 Timothy 3:16-17 states, "All Scripture is given by inspiration by God, and it is profitable for doctrine, for reproof, for correction, for instruction in righteousness that the man of God may be complete, thoroughly equipped for every good work.

We also must be doers of the Word and not merely hearers of it (Jas. 1:22). That is how you learn more about God and about His plans for your life.

All authors want you to read their book and God is no exception. He wrote the Bible and He wants you to read it.

It is not about religion, and it's not a collection of do's and don'ts. It is a personal love letter to you written in blood by an everlasting God who loves you.

It's about a personal relationship with the One who created you, loves you and died for you. He has done everything for you to come to Him, and He is waiting for you. The ball is in your court.

I've often thought about why the feelings of love, peace and acceptance were so powerful in my post-heart attack vision. I've come to understand why I felt His peace and love.

It's because Jesus is our Prince of Peace, our Shalom and He is Love, His love for us is unconditional, it is an agape love.

In Isaiah 9:6 He is described as "Wonderful, Counselor, Mighty God, Everlasting Father and Prince of Peace."

I also know that He is omniscient, omnipotent and omnipresent. I believe that someday we will each experience Jesus on a one-on-one basis. He is omnipresent.

He made us for fellowship with Him. Imagine, fellowship with Jesus for eternity?

I do not think heaven will take place entirely in group settings. I think we will experience Him completely as I did, one-on-one with the Lord for eternity.

When Jesus was crucified on the cross for our sins, He cried to the Father, "My God, My God, why have You forsaken Me?" (Mat. 27:47)

Jesus cried because His fellowship with the Father was over albeit for a brief moment.

In my post heart attack vision, why did He show such strong feelings of acceptance for me? Why did He want to show me that He accepts me? Why was that feeling of acceptance so prevalent in my vision?

He wanted to let me know that He accepts me and that He always has in spite of me. As Romans 5:8 states, "But God demonstrates His own love toward us, in that while we were still sinners, Christ died for us."

1 John 4:10 also says, "In this is love, not that we loved God, but that He loved us and sent His Son to be the propitiation for our sins."

God is still knocking at your door of your heart; will you answer His call? I trust and pray that you will.

CPSIA information can be obtained
at www.ICGtesting.com
Printed in the USA
FSHW010300280121
77990FS